THE
ANXIOUS
ECONOMY

Drawing by David Simpson
Courtesy *Tulsa Tribune*

THE
ANXIOUS
ECONOMY

Ezra Solomon
STANFORD UNIVERSITY

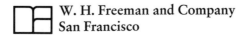 W. H. Freeman and Company
San Francisco

To Dr. Don F. Cameron
with affection and respect

Library of Congress Cataloging in Publication Data

Solomon, Ezra.
    The anxious economy.

    Includes bibliographical references.
    1.   United States—Economic conditions—
1961-   2.   Inflation (Finance)—United States.
I.   Title.
HC106.6.S65 1975   330.9'73'092   75-5560
ISBN 0-7167-0734-9
ISBN 0-7167-0735-7 pbk.

Printed in the United States of America

This book was published originally as a part of
The Portable Stanford, a series of books published
by the Stanford Alumni Association.

1   2   3   4   5   6   7   8   9

CONTENTS

CREDITS

PREFACE

The subject of this book is not economics as such, but rather the contemporary wave of economic problems and anxieties that afflicts us. Today, people and governments everywhere are seriously troubled by five anxieties:

1. Inflation and the prospect of more to come.
2. A worldwide recession and the fear that it might develop into a protracted depression.
3. Confusion in the international monetary system and the threat of a breakdown of the system itself.
4. The threat of shortages and the reality of huge price increases for raw materials, especially those related to energy.
5. Record high interest rates and a sharp fall in common stock prices here and elsewhere.

Explanations of how we got to where we are differ, and prescriptions for how we can return to more tranquil economic behavior differ even more. What follows is one economist's view of the nature of the problems and their solutions, written as simply as a complex and contentious subject allows.

The general theme of the book is that inflation is the central problem from which all of our other problems arise. Thus, in a sense, the book itself is about inflation—its causes, its manifestations, and its cure.

I have avoided footnotes as well as technical explanations in order to keep the flow of ideas as uncluttered as possible. When a new concept or measure is used that might require an explanation for someone unfamiliar with it, it is defined or explained briefly in the text. A brief Reader's Guide provides sources that deal with current economic developments.

Ezra Solomon

Stanford, California
December 15, 1974

DOWN AGAIN

Drawing by Chick Larsen
Courtesy *Richmond* (Va.) *Times–Dispatch*

CHAPTER ONE

THE U.S. ECONOMY
IN TRANSITION

IT IS PAINFUL, but useful, to begin by examining the principal anxieties which give the present book its title. As the economy has lurched from one crisis to another, the list of problems and anxieties has grown, and the interactions among them have become more complex.

Inflation. The basic problem, to which all of the other problems are somehow connected, is inflation. The U.S. and the rest of the world are suffering from what must be the lengthiest recorded bout of peacetime inflation. The inflation is occurring in spite of unprecedented attempts to control it; indeed it has worsened. In 1974, consumer prices in the U.S. rose by 12 percent in spite of a marked slowdown in economic activity, and far higher rates of price increases have been recorded elsewhere.

Recession or worse. Inflation itself and the attempts which have been made to curb it have led to a worldwide swing of the industrial economies into what threatens to be the most serious economic recession since World War II. The fear that further attempts to curb inflation will bring about a prolonged depression in economic activity is matched only by the fear that attempts to revive economic expansion will exacerbate the pace of inflation. The perceived gap between the Scylla of inflation and the Charybdis of depression has narrowed so markedly that many no longer see even the possibility of a safe passage between these two evils.

International monetary confusion. A third anxiety is that the international monetary order might collapse. The arrangement of fixed but alterable exchange rates, generally referred to as the Bretton Woods system, broke down in 1971 with the flight from the U.S. dollar, the key currency around which it was built. The dollar was devalued in late 1971 and again in early 1973. Since then all major exchange rates have been "floating" against each other for the first time in history. This in turn has created an atmosphere of uncertainty for many people and a vague feeling that a sense of order and stability is missing. Piled on top of all this the world now faces the trying "petro-dollar" question. The huge increase in the price of petroleum imposed by the major oil exporting countries since late 1973 requires a corresponding increase in payments by oil importing countries. As yet nobody knows for sure just how these vast international flows of money will be handled or indeed whether they *can* be handled within the existing monetary system.

Shortages. A fourth anxiety stems from the recent emergence of widespread shortages of basic raw materials, especially those related to food and energy, whose cheap and abundant supply we took for granted just a few years ago. The shortages have been accompanied by huge increases in most raw material prices.

Financial market behavior. The fifth and, for some segments of the population, the most painful of today's problems and anxieties is the behavior of interest rates and stock prices. Inflation, and the attempt to restrain it, brought about record high market interest rates in 1974. Home construction and public utility companies, which are peculiarly dependent on a cheap and plentiful supply of long-term financing, have suffered seriously because of their inability to compete for borrowed funds. The stock market fell sharply after early 1973, and by October 1974 stock prices were down to levels last seen in 1962. Given the huge fall in the purchasing power of the dollar, the *real* value of common stocks in October 1974 was actually down to levels prevailing nearly 20 years earlier.

The postwar world has experienced each of these present anxieties before, but one at a time and in one economy or another. What is new in the current situation is that all of the major economies are now afflicted by all of these problems. Taken together, they suggest to many that the orderly postwar era we have been living in has ended. In a sense it has. Until 1968 the U.S. took many things for granted, including:

1. That "supply" was not a major problem. Indeed, some of our policies, such as the artificially low ceiling placed on the price of natural gas and the restraints we placed on agricultural output, suggest that

some even believed that insuring adequate supply was not a problem at all.

2. That average living standards would automatically and continuously increase, so much so that we could eliminate poverty here and in the rest of the world; indeed, that we were so rich we could cure virtually any problem by spending enough money on it.

3. That all of those things could be accomplished without endangering either the price stability which we had also taken for granted, or the generally low level of interest rates to which we had become accustomed, or the external strength of the U.S. dollar, which we assumed was invulnerable.

4. That the stock market would keep rising forever, providing for investors a continuous hedge against whatever inflation might occur.

Obviously none of these comforting assumptions holds true today. The danger is not in giving them up—for they were not really valid in the first place. The danger rather is that we swing to the opposite extreme and assume that the most recent adversities will last forever. History and analysis both suggest that they will not. The central problem, and one from which all the others spring, is inflation. When that is durably corrected, most of the other problems will become more manageable. But the correction of inflation will require that we give it the same top priority we have hitherto given to other economic objectives, such as maximum growth, full employment, and income redistribution.

The unprecedented economic situation has been aggravated by unprecedented conditions of political instability and uncertainty. During a period in 1974 none of the major democracies had an effective majority government. In the U.S. itself, we experienced the potential impeachment and eventual resignation of the President. It is not surprising that surveys of consumer sentiment about the economy, which have been conducted systematically since the end of World War II, show that this index plunged to a record low level in 1974. Nor is it surprising that many people believe the U.S. economy is on the brink of a major crisis. That the economy is anxious is a fact. That it is in or headed for a major crisis is not equally true.

Crisis or Watershed?

Some years ago a group of newspaper sub-editors were discussing the most boring headlines they could think of. The winning entry was "Small Earthquake in Chile: Not Many Killed." Today, an opposite discussion of the most eye-catching headlines would no doubt see many an entry with the word *crisis* in it. It has become the custom to call almost everything a crisis these days. In recent years we have had a whole series of international monetary crises, several food crises, an energy crisis, and a liquidity crisis. The custom helps to sell newspapers and books, especially if the book also promises to tell the reader how to get rich when the crisis comes.

The use of the word crisis for recent economic events is misleading in two ways. It exaggerates the nature of the event being described. For example, in spite of crisis after crisis, international trade and exchange have not collapsed, nor have we run out of meat, toilet paper, or gasoline. More importantly, the word crisis wrongly implies that a clearcut turning point is at hand at which time matters will get dramatically better or dramatically worse. Fortunately or unfortunately, economic events develop far less rapidly or clearly than the word crisis suggests. In fact they develop painfully slowly.

Most of the events that have made the headlines recently had been brewing for many years before they burst in front of the public's attention. Their resolution will also take time.

For example, the Bretton Woods system—as the postwar international monetary system was called—did not fall apart in one sharp crisis on August 15, 1971, when the U.S. officially suspended the right of foreign central banks to convert their holdings of dollars into gold on demand. The system had been slowly falling apart for years prior to that date. Indeed the expanding volume of dollars held by foreign central banks first exceeded the total value of gold held by the U.S. Treasury back in 1964. With that event it was clear to everybody by 1965 that convertibility of these holdings into gold was a hypothetical rather than a practical right.

In short, the old system did not die; it faded away gradually over the course of several years. Nor, as many expected, did a new "system" arise full-blown from some blueprint developed at an international conference. A new system will emerge gradually—and indeed it has already begun to do so—but it will be years before its shape settles down enough for someone to give it a name.

Much the same is true for the other major problems that underlie today's anxieties. Inflation, shortages, high interest rates, weak stock prices have all been developing since at least as far back as 1965. Correcting those problems is going to take a period of years rather than months. Correcting them in a context of a deepening recession is going to take a combination of courage, skill, and luck that few people are willing to attribute to Washington.

Nobody in this generation is going to be able to point a finger at one date or event which marks a critical turning point. However, if what we have been experiencing is not a "crisis," the concurrence of so many basic problems and manifestations does suggest that we are passing through a major watershed in U.S. economic history, at least as important as that marked by World War II.

It is convenient to divide time into identifiable periods. The decade provides one such basis for minor punctuation. It has become a ritual at the start of each new decade to program speeches by economists dealing with prospects for the ten-year period ahead. It has also become the ritual for public relations men to jazz up and alliterate the usually drab titles assigned by economists to these talks. Thus we had the "fabulous fifties"—and in a sense the decade deserved that extravagant title: the widespread fear of a postwar depression evaporated, the flurry of inflation associated with the Korean War rapidly wound down, the stock market climbed to levels fully commensurate with the economy's new size and prosperity. Even today the year 1955 stands out as one in which the U.S. economy best realized its dream of full, non-inflationary peacetime prosperity.

The favorite adjective for the 1960s was "soaring." For most of that decade the description did fit. The pace of economic expansion accelerated, prices remained relatively stable, and common stock prices more than doubled between 1955 and 1965. Finding an appropriate title in 1970 was more difficult. (In spite of the quirk in our calendar which sets the proper beginning of each decade at years which end with the numeral *one*, it is the custom to schedule the kind of speech I am referring to in years ending with the numeral *zero*.) A few people went along with "stupendous" or "super." For my part I suppressed the compulsion for alliteration to stay with a more sober title, "The Economy in Transition." Looking back from the decade's halfway point, I now see that I was right, but could have given the public relations man his way by adding a subtitle: "The Sobering Seventies." (Some people, more affected by the current wave of disillusionment, might prefer words like sorry, sad, sour, or seething.)

The thought that the economy is undergoing a sobering and lengthy transition invites the idea of even longer sub-periods in its history. In this century, the German army has conveniently provided two larger punctuation points than those which mark each decade; World War I and World War II are both major watersheds. It now appears that the Vietnam War and its aftermath mark yet another major watershed in twentieth-century economic history. What we have called the "postwar" period came to an end in the late sixties or early seventies. The economy is now in transition to a new period. Whatever it comes to be called (post-Vietnam?), the period we have entered is likely to reflect patterns of economic behavior, attitudes, and policies that will differ from the post-World War II decades as significantly as those years differed from the decades prior to World War II. These differences will affect the domestic economy as well as our international economic relationships.

External Economic Relations

We have already witnessed major transitions in our external economic relationships. A large number of significant events took place in 1971. The U.S. substantially completed its withdrawal of troops from Vietnam. It also began the shift from a policy of Cold War to one of accommodation. On the economic side of events, we imposed a temporary surcharge on imports to protect our domestic industry, suspended the right of foreign central banks to convert the dollars they held, and later in the year devalued the dollar. These events marked an end to conditions and policies that had prevailed for the quarter-century following the end of World War II.

Postwar foreign policy. During those 25 years, U.S. international economic policy had been essentially a "stepchild" of U.S. foreign policy, which in turn had been a captive of the Cold War. The highlights of our postwar policies were as follows:

1. After World War II ended, the U.S. made a significant and successful effort to rebuild the economies of Western Europe and Japan, to encourage the development of the European Common Market, to foster the free international exchange of goods, services, and capital, and to stimulate the flow of aid to Third World countries—especially those on the rim of the Iron Curtain.

2. As part of this effort, the U.S. kept the Bretton Woods system alive by its willingness and ability to sustain almost continuous balance of payments deficits. Throughout the 1950s, the rest of the free world had a strong need to rebuild its fund of internationally acceptable cash reserves; the only medium through which they could achieve that purpose was the accumulation of U.S. dollars. The U.S. itself was a major net exporter of goods and services during most of the period and hence a potential net gainer of dollars on trade account. However, the U.S. was wise and generous enough to encourage and permit a sufficiently large outflow of dollars to satisfy the rest of the world's demand for an increasing stock of U.S. dollars. We did this by opening our doors to imports, by permitting freedom of travel and tourism, and by creating a large flow of gifts, loans, and investments to overseas areas. The excellent results achieved were due, in part, to the willingness of the United States to permit strong currencies, such as the West German

mark and the Japanese yen, to remain significantly undervalued relative to the dollar, and to our acquiescence in allowing weaker currencies to devalue at will.

3. A third aspect of international policy between 1945 and 1970 was our severe restriction on trade with the Soviet Union, the People's Republic of China, and Cuba.

Changing conditions in foreign policy. The conditions which led to those policies, and the policies themselves, have changed dramatically:

1. The U.S. is no longer the preeminent economic power it was in the early 1950s. The European Economic Community, now enlarged, and Japan are both commensurable superpowers as far as industrial production is concerned.

2. The balance of relative financial strength also changed dramatically during the late 1960s. The foreign appetite for accumulating U.S. dollars was satisfied by 1970. Indeed, 1971 marked a flight *from* the dollar *to* other stronger currencies, notably the mark, the yen, the Swiss franc, and the Dutch guilder. The purposeful postwar overvaluation of the dollar, which had served a perceived need during the 1950s and 1960s, now required correction, with the value of the dollar readjusted downward. To achieve that, the U.S. dollar was devalued twice: first in 1971 and again early in 1973. Even so, its external value continued to sink in the now freed or "floating" market for foreign exchange, reaching a low point in July 1973.

3. U.S. trade policy also shifted in response to the changing balance of relative economic strength. We imposed a temporary import surcharge in 1971 to protect both the dollar and our ability to compete in home markets. We bargained strenuously for better access for U.S. products to foreign markets and for some degree of insulation of U.S. markets against rapidly rising foreign competition.

4. The Cold War itself gave way to accommodation with the Soviet Union and China, and more recently with Cuba. Trade relationships with these economies have been encouraged.

5. The huge increases in the price of petroleum and other raw materials have reversed the balance of economic power between the industrial societies and the nations which own those raw materials. Closer economic, financial, and diplomatic ties with raw material producers, and especially with the Arab nations, have been restored.

In brief, the postwar primacy of foreign policy *over* international economic policy is in the process of being reversed. During the final quarter of the present century, U.S. foreign policy may well become the stepchild of U.S. international economic interests.

The Domestic Economy

Developments within the domestic economy are neither as clearcut nor as visible as they are in our foreign relations, but they are likely to be equally profound. To understand the nature of the transition from the postwar era in which we have been living, we must first understand the ideas and policies which shaped the era itself.

The U.S. came out of World War II fearing a return to the depressed economic conditions of the 1930s. The national economic attitude in 1945 was characterized by its determination on two issues:

1. It would avoid the traumatic experience of depression and high unemployment that it had suffered during the decade prior to World War II.

2. In order to achieve that, it would apply the still untested tools of economic policy advocated by what was then called the "New Economics"—the amendments to economic theory and policy put forward by John Maynard Keynes and his followers during the 1930s.

The first resolve is easy enough to understand. The decade of the 1930s was, without exception, the worst decade in U.S. economic experience. The unemployment rate reached 25 percent of the labor force in 1933, and it *averaged* nearly 20 percent for the entire 10-year period 1931-40.

Until 1930 growth, and confidence in our further ability to grow, had been implicit assumptions of U.S. economic life. Early visions of a single continental economy running from ocean to ocean, of 100 million people producing 100 million tons of steel a year, of unlimited immigration, land-grant colleges, and universal education—all were highly growth-oriented concepts. The 1930s dealt a bitter blow to those hopes and assumptions. In 1939, total U.S. output was smaller than it had been in 1929, nearly 10 million people were unemployed, the birth rate had fallen to the lowest level recorded (under 19 per thousand), immigration had dwindled, and the common stock indexes were still more than 50 percent below the average level attained in 1929.

The New Economics: The Keynesian Revolution

The prescription for high employment and growth put forward by the New Economics requires a longer explanation. In retrospect, the essential message of the Keynesian "revolution," as it came to be called, was fairly simple. Basically, it said:

1. In a modern economy, the level of economic activity is *limited* by its supply capacity, but it is not *determined* by supply power alone.

Jean Carlu. Collection, The Museum of Modern Art, New York.
Gift of the Office of Emergency Management.

Within the limit of supply, the actual level of output and employment is determined by the total demand for goods and services, frequently referred to by economists as "aggregate" or "effective" or "total" demand.

2. The level of aggregate demand can and may fall short of a nation's aggregate or total supply capacity, and thus lead to rising unemployment and sluggish growth. Furthermore, a condition of inadequate demand, as well as its undesirable consequences, could persist unless something were done about it.

3. Inadequate total demand can and should be corrected by deliberately applying fiscal stimulus to the economy—either by expanding government spending (without raising taxes) or by cutting taxes (without reducing spending) or by doing both.

The volume of controversy unleashed by Keynes' ideas probably fills more shelves in the economic sections of libraries than any other single subject in the field. An entire issue of one learned journal devoted itself to reviews of his book—an unprecedented occurrence even for academia. The many reasons for the extended controversy over Keynesian economics are of interest only to historians of economic thought. Some of the controversies still continue today, 40 years later. But one aspect of the debate is relevant for present purposes, and that concerns the relative priorities that national economic theory and policy assign to aggregate *supply* on the one hand and aggregate *demand* on the other.

The mainstream of economic thought had argued, quite correctly, that supply capacity was the key to the economic well-being of nations. Since human wants are almost unlimited, it was assumed that in the aggregate, demand would always be sufficient to absorb the output produced by a fully-employed economy operating at its capacity. Admittedly, part of that productive capacity—either labor or capital or both—would sometimes become unemployed because of lack of demand for specific forms of output or labor. But that development, it was assumed, would be corrected (and should be corrected) by a fall in the relative price or wage of the unemployed elements until it became feasible once again for them to be reemployed. In brief, for classical economists the concept of aggregate demand was not an important variable for either theory or policy.

The classical view on the unimportance of aggregate demand had been challenged many times before Keynes, but mainly by people outside the mainstream of economic thought, and never successfully. One early economist who worried about the recessionary problems that could be caused by inadequate aggregate demand was the Reverend Thomas Malthus, the first person in England to hold a professorial title in Political Economy, as the subject was then called. But Malthus was never quite able to show how a shortfall in aggregate demand could occur in the first place.

The orthodox counter-argument to Malthus was that people join the labor force or work longer hours only because they want goods and services; therefore each increase in the aggregate output is always preceded by an increase in potential demand. Furthermore, the process of producing output generates an equal flow of income, which allows the rise in potential demand to become translated into actual demand. The act of *supply*, so to speak, creates its own *demand*.

In any case, Malthus, who must have been a chronic worrier, spent most of his best writing on an opposite worry—namely that the growth in aggregate demand would outrun aggregate supply capacity. That worry is better recognized as his celebrated theory that population growth would outstrip the ability of production to grow, so that man's inescapable fate was poverty.

Both of Malthus' theories, or worries, were rejected not only in his own lifetime, but for a whole century after his death. Both theories have since been resuscitated. Keynes paid him tribute for his pioneering perceptions regarding the crucial importance of aggregate or effective demand. More recently, the Club of Rome has revived his other idea, as well as the essential methodology he used, to show that uncontrolled growth must eventually lead to the impoverishment of society.

We are here concerned only with Keynes' development of aggregate or effective demand as a key variable in national economic analysis and policy. Unlike Malthus, Keynes was not a maverick. He was the son of a well-known economist, heir apparent to what was then the world's most distinguished chair in economics, and the author of significant and orthodox milestones in the field. In spite of intense controversy, his ideas soon had a large following within the profession. The events of the 1930s themselves seemed to support his argument that a lack of adequate demand could bring a modern economy to a state of serious underemployment and keep it there indefinitely.

However, no Western government applied the cure Keynes recommended—a bold and deliberate creation of aggregate demand through fiscal policy. The world of the mid-1930s was not yet ready for the idea that a consciously engineered fiscal deficit was the correct or safe way to cure a depression. Then came World War II. The war inadvertently brought into being fiscal stimulation even more massive than anything Keynes had envisaged. Both the depression and unemployment which had persisted for 10 years disappeared rapidly and output rose sharply. Table 1 tells the story well.

Table 1: Selected Economic Data, 1929, 1939, & 1946

	1929	1939	1946
Gross private product* (billions of 1958 $)	191.0	189.0	275.0
Labor Force (millions)	49.4	55.6	61.0
Total Civilian Employment (millions)	47.6	45.7	55.3
Total Employment (millions)	47.9	46.1	58.7
Unemployment (millions)	1.6	9.5	2.3
Unemployment Rate (percent)	3.2	17.2	3.9

* Gross private product equals gross national product *excluding* the output of government employees.

Postwar Economic Policy

Postwar economic policy was based on two Keynesian premises: (1) that aggregate demand is a crucial determinant of the level of output and employment; and (2) that it is the continuing responsibility of the government to use all practicable means in its power, including monetary and fiscal policies, to keep aggregate demand high enough to ensure maximum employment and economic activity.

Along with many Western democracies, all of whom shared the same fear of a return to the "terrible thirties," the U.S. passed legislation enshrining high employment as a major official objective. The Employment Act of 1946 committed the U.S. government to "use all practicable means . . . to promote maximum employment, production, and purchasing power." The same Act established the Council of Economic Advisers in the Executive Office of the President, set up a joint Senate-House Economic Committee, and promulgated the practice of regular economic reports to the Congress by the President and the Council.

The postwar quest for high employment, fast growth, and a recession-free economy was highly successful—not just in the U.S. but in other industrial societies as well. The top priority we assigned to those three related objectives did provide us with a high pay-off in terms of results. The deep postwar recession which many expected in the late forties did not occur. Between 1946 and 1968, the economy performed vastly better than it had during the 22-year interwar period between 1919 and 1941 and better even than its performance during the 22 years prior to World War I. As Table 2 shows, between 1946 and 1968 recessions were milder, real growth was faster, and unemployment lower than we experienced either between 1919 and 1941 or between 1892 and 1914.

Table 2: Economic Performance: Selected 22-Year Periods 1892-1968
(Percent Per Annum Rates)

	Pre-WWI 1892-1914	Interwar 1919-1941	Postwar 1946-1968
Real growth of GNP	3.2	2.7	3.8
Average unemployment rate	7.3	11.1	4.6
Highest unemployment rate (& year)	18.5 (1894)	25.0 (1933)	6.8 (1958)
Fraction of period in recession	49.0	37.0	16.0
Change in consumer prices	+0.3	−0.7	+2.6

Postwar policy did not give a high priority to the maintenance of price stability. Price stability as such was not mentioned in the Employment Act of 1946, although during the Eisenhower years the phrase "maximum purchasing power" was interpreted as a mandate for that objective. Attempts were made to amend the act in order to give maximum price stability a legal priority equal to that enjoyed by maximum employment and maximum output, but they did not succeed.

Price performance between 1946 and 1968 was clearly not as good as it had been in earlier periods: from 1892 to 1914 the price level was essentially stable; from 1919 to 1941 average prices actually declined; from 1946 to 1968 prices rose on average by about 2.6 percent per year. That rise was not in itself alarming. A flurry of price increases followed the removal of controls after World War II and another occurred during the Korean War, but both episodes were short-lived. A third, and more troublesome, wave of price increases began in 1956 just when the economy was enjoying its first peacetime year of full employment, but this was corrected by the recession of 1958 and a temporary sacrifice of fast growth.

Apart from those brief episodes, the average postwar year experienced a modest upward creep of prices at about 1.5 percent a year. Given the nation's preference for growth, the modest price rise was regarded as tolerable, especially since it had very little adverse effect either on the ability of mortgage and capital markets to raise large sums for debt financing or on the strong rise in common stock prices from 1949 to 1968.

The "New Economics" finally came of age, and the concept of an expansionary economic policy enjoyed its greatest success, during the first half of the 1960s. President Kennedy had succeeded to office committed to accelerated growth and the achievement of full employment—in his words, "to getting the country moving again." The period 1958-60, as we have seen, had temporarily downplayed those (by now traditional) objectives in order to curb the small wave of inflation which struck the economy in 1956 and 1957.

The highly expansionary economic policies initiated in early 1961 were a great success. The economy expanded rapidly between 1961 and 1965; unemployment declined, slowly at first but by early 1965 it was below 5 percent. After six years of almost no growth between 1955 and 1961, corporate profits were up by well over 50 percent by 1965, and business capital expenditures rose even more rapidly. Furthermore, the rate of inflation remained at a modest level of 1.5 percent a year, about the same as it had been in 1960 before the expansionary policies of the Kennedy-Johnson years were instituted. After 1965 the first signs of economic problems began to appear, and those problems are still with us.

The steady and heady success of postwar economic policy and the New Economics led to a rapid accumulation of unrealistic assumptions, attitudes, and actions, which eventually led the economy into trouble.

Policy Targets

The original Keynesian innovation was the simple and correct assertion that "for the economy as a whole aggregate demand is *also* important." It took nearly two decades for that simple idea to displace the century-old, but incorrect, tradition that "only aggregate supply is important." But once the new idea prevailed, the emphasis of thinking and policy moved quickly to the opposite extreme. The original Keynesian idea that demand is *also* important gave way to the somewhat different idea that demand is *more* important and finally to the totally different idea that, in a rich economy like the U.S., supply could be taken for granted! The shift in emphasis showed up clearly in the policies we pursued during the latter half of the 1960s:

1. We adopted policies which kept increasing the total demand for goods and services. For example, in 1965, with the economy already operating at close to its full normal capacity, we simultaneously embarked on a costly war in Vietnam and on an equally costly war on poverty without bothering to increase taxes in order to pay for either venture.

2. We also pursued a set of numerous less visible but important policies which had the effect of suppressing rather than encouraging supply. For example, to keep consumers happy we placed unrealistically low price ceilings on natural gas, which led to a serious fall in the level of exploratory and drilling efforts and eventually to shortages; to keep farmers happy we paid them *not* to expand production; to keep a whole lot of people happy, including environmentalists, we placed increasingly

onerous restraints on the construction of new production facilities and the institution of more productive methods; to satisfy our quest for a more egalitarian society we imposed larger tax burdens on work and economic success even as we increased the rewards for not working.

As a result of these policies, and the way in which they were financed through large budget deficits, the level of total demand ran ahead of our capacity to supply—which in turn triggered the long and worsening inflation we have experienced since 1965 as well as the other basic dilemmas we face today.

Beyond the Watershed

If the economy is indeed at a major watershed, can economics explain how we got to where we are or speculate intelligently about where we go from here?

For some people the answer is "No"—we are where we are because the laws of economics do not work anymore. Inflation worsens even as the economy slumps; wage demands accelerate in the face of mounting unemployment; stock prices decline to new lows even as the price of everything else jumps to a new high. For these people the prescription is clear. We have to rewrite the economic textbooks and refashion our basic economic arrangements to suit the new realities. Others, in a similar mood, hope that some new theorist will turn up (a "new Keynes," as *Business Week* calls him) with a new theory that will tell us how we can get back to a world in which we can once again enjoy the simultaneous assurance of rapid growth, low unemployment, rising incomes, stable prices, low interest rates, high stock prices, and an abundant and inexpensive supply of energy and other raw materials.

There is also a large body of opinion which holds that we do not need to rewrite economics at all, but to reread the subject, especially the ideas contained in the introductory chapter!

One of America's great economists, Frank Knight of the University of Chicago, used to say that the essential message of economics can be summarized in one sentence: For society as a whole there is no such thing as a free lunch. He was right, and that is why economics has been called the dismal science. Every economic policy action has a cost; we can achieve one set of priorities only by sacrificing another. After 1965 the U.S. behaved *as if* there might be a free lunch after all, and we are now suffering the consequences of that behavior.

While there are no easy answers or quick solutions to the mess of economic problems which give rise to today's anxieties, what has occurred is neither mysterious nor irreversible.

As Knight's dictum indicates, economics is essentially a matter of

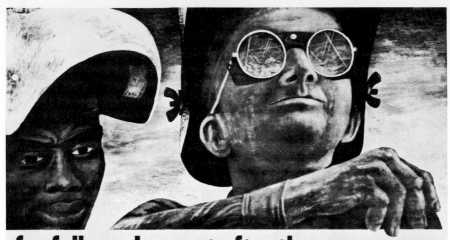

for full employment after the war
REGISTER VOTE
CIO POLITICAL ACTION COMMITTEE

Ben Shahn. Collection, The Museum of Modern Art, New York.
Gift of the CIO Political Action Committee.

priorities—to get something in a world of scarce resources it is usually necessary to give up something else. Postwar U.S. economic policy placed its highest priorities on the pursuit of maximum growth in demand, on minimum unemployment, and on the quest for ways to redistribute real income to selected groups in society. At least until 1965 our economic policy did well *because* of that emphasis. After 1965 we added other items to the high priority list—one was military and the other environmental. In the process still other objectives were shortchanged, notably price stability, the external value of the dollar, and the incentives for expanding our basic capacity to supply the goods and services required by our rapidly expanding expectations for even more. The predictable results were inflation, devaluation, a collapse of the old international monetary system, and threatened shortages of essential raw materials. None of these had been thought of as a serious potential threat during most of the postwar period. Even worse, the rapid emergence of serious problems in these previously neglected areas eventually led to equally serious problems even in the areas to which postwar policy had assigned its highest priorities. By the end of 1974 the economy had moved into a serious recession, unemployment had increased rapidly, and inflation had erased most of the economic gains made by the relatively poor and disadvantaged groups in society.

Given these bitter lessons, economic policy and performance beyond the present watershed are likely to be significantly different from what we experienced during the postwar period which ended in the late 1960s:

1. There will be far less emphasis on boosting aggregate demand in order to stimulate economic growth and reduce the rate of unemployment. There will be far greater emphasis on reachieving acceptable price stability and on dealing with the problem of unemployment by more direct means such as public employment programs, apprenticeship and training programs, and income maintenance programs.

2. More emphasis will be devoted to increasing the supply side of the economic equation, and especially in the areas of food and energy. That emphasis will include inducements as well as the removal of unnecessary existing barriers to productivity.

3. Finally, the rapid rise in the *share* of the public sector (federal, state, and local) in the economy will be halted.

The Budget

The budget is the major vehicle through which economic and social policy operates. The rough picture I have sketched for the period beyond the present watershed assumes that the rapid postwar expansion of non-defense spending (which has risen twice as fast as the economy has over the past 20 years) will be brought under stricter control. The logic for this assumption is that a continuing *rise* in the government's share of national output (especially when financed by deficits) is highly inflationary and that inflation must be convincingly halted before the economy can return to normal again.

Given the changing composition of the Congress toward the liberal side of the aisle, my assumption of more restrained budgets in the future may strike many readers as an unrealistic one. But many lessons in history suggest that it is not as unrealistic as it might at first appear. It took a Tory Prime Minister, Robert Peel, to get rid of the British tariff on wheat in 1846 even though the conventional posture of his political party was strongly against that move. It took America's leading anti-Communist to open the door to China. When logic suggests a major move, it is likely to happen even if it conflicts with conventional postures. The need to correct inflation and its consequences by getting governmental budgets under better control over the next five years is now so great it will have to be done. Indeed, the folk hero of the coming decade may well be a liberal Democrat who succeeds in balancing the budget again!

THE MAN WHO CAME TO DINNER

PERMANENT INFLATION

Drawing by Bruce Shanks
Courtesy *Buffalo Evening News*

4-17-73

CHAPTER TWO

INFLATION AND ITS CAUSES

FUTURE HISTORY BOOKS will undoubtedly refer to 1974 as the year of the Great Inflation. In the U.S., consumer prices rose at a rate of 12 percent a year. Elsewhere, with the exception of West Germany, the rates of inflation experienced in 1974 ranged upward from that in the U.S.: 14 percent in France, 18 percent in the United Kingdom, and 25 percent in Japan.

The U.S., like most other major countries, had suffered serious inflation in the past, but mainly in wartime. U.S. consumer prices rose almost 80 percent during the Civil War. However, after 1865 the price level fell gradually for the rest of the century. Inflation was also serious during and immediately after World War I; from 1915 to 1920 consumer prices almost doubled. But again, after 1920 prices subsided for two decades until the outbreak of World War II. Inflation associated with the Second World War saw consumer prices rise by 72 percent between 1940 and 1948. This time, however, the subsequent pattern of events was different. Apart from a mild decline in 1949, consumer prices continued to rise, fairly sharply during the Korean War years 1950-53 and then at a steady creep of about $1\frac{1}{2}$ percent a year between 1953 and 1965.

The present and latest bout of inflation began with U.S. military involvement in Vietnam in 1965. The pre-Vietnam inflation rate of $1\frac{1}{2}$

PERCENTAGE CHANGE IN CONSUMER PRICES 1860-1973

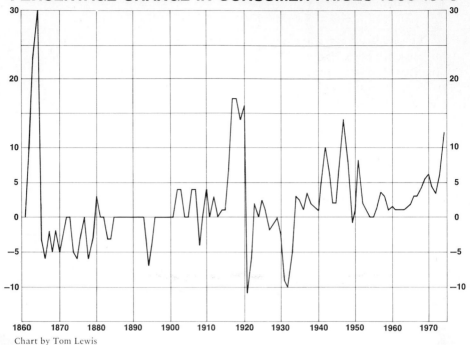

Chart by Tom Lewis

percent doubled to 3 percent in 1966 and 1967, then redoubled to 6 percent in 1969 and 1970. Helped by a lull in economic activity and the imposition of direct wage and price controls, the inflation rate abated to the $3\frac{1}{2}$ percent level during 1972. But starting at the end of 1972, prices began to accelerate. By 1974 the inflation rate in the U.S. redoubled once again to 12 percent per annum, twice the 1970 rate. Furthermore, by 1974 the Great Inflation was clearly a worldwide problem.

What causes inflation? What particular mix of causes influenced the course of events between 1965 and 1974? Like other people, most economists have a natural preference for a single, tidy way of explaining events. However, the inflation we have been experiencing since 1965 is not a single, tidy phenomenon. Different forces have been at work during different sub-periods, and no single theory can adequately explain all that has happened. Nonetheless, the attempt to find a single "best" theory for all forms of inflation leads to different schools of thought and endless intramural debates among them—all of which confuses laymen as much as it delights the academics.

The Monetary Explanation

The preferred explanation for inflation places primary emphasis on the presence of excessive demand caused by an excessive increase in the quantity of money. Indeed, the original definition of the word *inflation* refers to the rapid enlargement of the money supply. We now use the term to refer to the result of that enlargement, namely a rapid increase in the price level. The simple version is "too much money chasing too few goods."

If one looks at all of the historical inflations in all of the countries in which the phenomenon has occurred, the monetary explanation wins hands down as the best single explanation available. For most episodes it is the *only* explanation required. For all episodes, an excess of monetary demand is at least a necessary condition for inflation, although in some situations it may not be the only factor at work.

Expansion of the money supply clearly played a large part in generating the inflation we, and the rest of the world, have been suffering. Any comparison of the growth in the money supply and the rise in consumer prices over the past two decades shows that the two have moved together. From 1955 to 1964 the money supply rose at 2.0 percent a year. From 1965 to 1970 money growth accelerated to 5.2 percent. From 1970 to mid-1974 it accelerated further to 6.7 percent. The rise in consumer prices behaved in similar fashion. From 1955 to 1964 prices rose at 1.6 percent a year. They accelerated to 4.2 percent between 1965 and 1970 and from 1970 to mid-1974 accelerated further to 5.7 percent in spite of partial suppression by wage and price controls during part of the period.

While the orthodox monetary theory of inflation is essentially correct, it is not complete. It does not, in itself, provide a full explanation for the long and accelerating inflation we have been experiencing. Too many questions are left unanswered:

1. If excess demand, created by an excessive increase in the stock of money, is the prime cause of inflation, the prevention or cure of inflation must lie in monetary restraint. Yet, in spite of a recognized worldwide need to prevent or reduce inflation, how is it that responsible governments and central bankers, year after year, are unable to administer that simple remedy?

2. Why did U.S. inflation persist, indeed worsen, in 1969 and 1970, even after the principal sources of excessive demand were removed following the end of 1968? Why did inflation worsen so rapidly in 1974 in spite of the general softening of demand and economic activity?

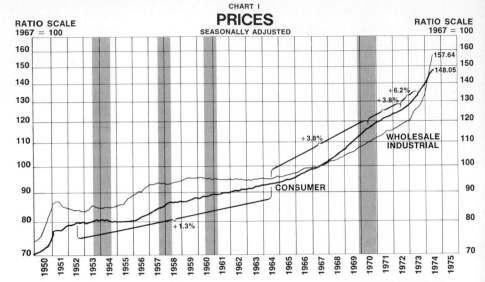

CHART I
PRICES
SEASONALLY ADJUSTED

RATIO SCALE
1967 = 100

RATIO SCALE
1967 = 100

157.64
148.05
+6.2%
+3.8%
+3.8%
WHOLESALE
INDUSTRIAL
CONSUMER
+1.3%

SHADED AREAS REPRESENT PERIODS OF BUSINESS RECESSIONS AS DEFINED BY THE NATIONAL BUREAU OF
ECONOMIC RESEARCH.
PERCENTAGES ARE ANNUAL RATES OF CHANGE FOR PERIODS INDICATED.
LATEST DATA PLOTTED: JULY

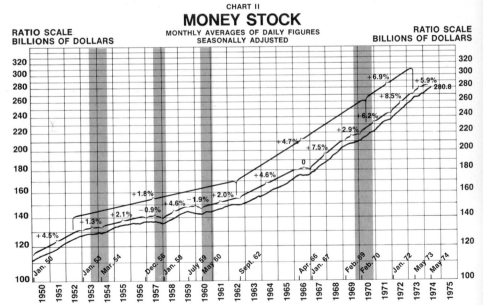

CHART II
MONEY STOCK
MONTHLY AVERAGES OF DAILY FIGURES
SEASONALLY ADJUSTED

RATIO SCALE
BILLIONS OF DOLLARS

RATIO SCALE
BILLIONS OF DOLLARS

+6.9%
+5.9%
280.8
+8.5%
+6.2%
+2.9%
+4.7%
+7.5%
0
+4.6%
+1.8%
+2.0%
+4.6%
−1.9%
−0.9%
+2.1%
−1.3%
+4.5%

Jan. 50
Jan. 53
Mar. 54
Dec. 56
Jan. 58
July 59
May 60
Sept. 62
Apr. 66
Jan. 67
Feb. 69
Feb. 70
Jan. 72
May 73
May 74

SHADED AREAS REPRESENT PERIODS OF BUSINESS RECESSIONS AS DEFINED BY THE NATIONAL BUREAU OF
ECONOMIC RESEARCH.
PERCENTAGES ARE ANNUAL RATES OF CHANGE FOR PERIODS INDICATED.
LATEST DATA PLOTTED: AUGUST

Data from Federal Reserve Bank of St. Louis, September 1974 *Review*.
Charts by Tom Lewis

3. During the second half of 1972 the pace of inflation subsided to 3.6 percent a year. Since then the U.S. monetary supply has grown at 6.2 percent a year—admittedly an excessive rate. But how can this fact alone explain the doubling, tripling, and indeed quadrupling in the prices of so many key commodities such as grain, sugar, petroleum, and many metals? How can it explain the two-digit rate of rise in general consumer prices or the 20-30 percent rate of increase in wholesale prices?

The Influence of Fiscal Policy. To explain the inflation we have experienced it is necessary to look at factors that lie beneath and beyond the money supply itself. One important factor is the behavior of fiscal policy.

Prior to the 1930s, the traditional viewpoint on fiscal policy was that, except in extraordinary circumstances such as war, the government should balance its budget, year in and year out. An increase in expenditure should be matched by a corresponding tax increase; a cut in tax rates should be matched by a corresponding cut in spending.

The Keynesian revolution showed us that fiscal policy should be administered in a more active fashion. In this view the budget should be actively used to provide stimulus to an economy when stimulus is necessary (i.e., when productive resources are unemployed) or to serve as a brake when the economy is expanding too rapidly (i.e., when upward price pressures are strong). Fiscal stimulus can be provided either by increasing the level of government spending or by cutting taxes or by doing both—in short, by running a budget deficit. Likewise, fiscal restraint can be applied by running a budget which is in surplus, and this surplus can in turn be achieved by cutting expenditures, raising tax rates, or both.

Fiscal policy has direct as well as indirect effects on the economy. For example, a stimulative policy (a budget deficit) directly increases the level of aggregate demand, because the government is spending more each year than it is receiving via taxation. The budget deficit also has an important indirect effect via its influence on the growth of money supply.

The kind of influence exerted by a budget deficit depends on how the deficit is financed. If the deficit is financed entirely by issuing new government debt to households (e.g., through the sale of savings bonds) the monetary effect is small. What happens is that idle money balances previously held by households are now borrowed and spent by the government. In other words, the quantity of money remains unchanged but its velocity, or average rate of circulation, is increased. However, the government can also finance the deficit by borrowing from the banking system. If that is done, and it frequently *is* done, it will automatically produce an increase in the supply of money. This increase in turn tends to stimulate private spending some time later. In short, large budget deficits can have a powerful *expansionary effect* on the money supply.

Countervailing influences: the Federal Reserve System. The pure monetarist would argue that the central banking authority (i.e., the Federal Reserve System) can offset the fiscally induced increase in the stock of money through countervailing monetary policies. But this argument ignores political and economic realities. If the Administration and the Congress use fiscal policy for the purpose of stimulating the economy, it is unlikely that the Central Bank can or will interpose its own judgment to frustrate that objective. There are of course occasions when fiscal policy is *inadvertently* stimulating because Congress does not have the will or the political courage to cut spending or raise tax rates. In such instances, the Central Bank may step in to offset some of the monetary side effects of the fiscal deficit. But such countervailing action cannot be pushed too far because it tends to produce heavy strains in the private credit market, especially in mortgage credit. The reason for the strain is as follows: If total credit availability is held down by the Central Bank during a period in which the government's need for credit is large or rising (because the deficit is large or growing), the availability of credit for private needs must shrink. Private competition for that shrinking supply of credit leads to a sharp tightening in the credit markets (banks and other lending institutions) and sometimes to sharp increases in interest rates—a condition that has come to be known as a "credit crunch."

Thus a stimulative fiscal policy and budget deficits generally tend to be accompanied by and indeed in part work because they induce a growth in the supply of money.

The Socio-Political Explanation

The postwar discovery that fiscal policy can and should be used as a policy instrument for stimulating or restraining the economy has had a major effect on the course of events since World War II. The idea of a compensatory fiscal policy—the use of fiscal policy as an accelerator or a brake—is in itself a neutral one. But the way it came to be used, especially after 1960, was not neutral. For three separate reasons it was used with great frequency as an *accelerator* and only rarely as a *brake*.

1. **The policy bias.** As indicated in Chapter One, postwar U.S. policy, especially after 1960, placed a heavy and sometimes exclusive priority on the objectives of fast growth and full employment. That emphasis was a reaction to the miserable performance of the U.S. economy and the cruel level of unemployment during the 1930s. The high priority placed on expansion and full employment after World War II led nat-

urally to a bias in favor of stimulative fiscal policy. The relevance of that bias for inflation is clear enough. Prices and wages tend to rise when the economy is operating close to the zone of its full capacity. Insofar as fiscal stimulus kept pushing us toward full capacity utilization, it created conditions in which there would tend to be strong upward pressures on prices and wages.

In contrast, prices and wages tend to soften, or even to decline, only when the flow of total demand for goods and labor falls below the level of total potential supply. Such a situation implies that part of the nation's supply capacity, including the labor force, is not fully employed. Without the intervention of an external force, the unemployed resources can, in fact, become fully employed only by lowering the price of goods or the wage rate. However, given the high priority placed on maximum growth and full employment, the government steps in with stimulative fiscal measures whenever economic growth falters and the unemployment rate rises. In the process, the conduct of government policy itself removes conditions conducive to a fall in prices and wages and creates conditions conducive to their future increase.

Clearly, the expansionary bias implicit in postwar policy objectives is one basic reason for the string of large deficits we have had over the past 15 years, as well as for the growing rate of monetary expansion we have experienced since 1965. The uninterrupted rise in prices since 1949 is a result of those developments—as is the acceleration of inflation since 1965.

2. **The political bias.** The political bias requires less explanation than the policy bias discussed above. It is far easier in our system for the government to vote for an increase in expenditures or a cut in tax rates than to do either of the opposite things. The number of special interest groups is both large and growing. No group, to my knowledge, has ever advocated either a relative or an absolute increase in its own taxes. Nor has any group advocated a cut in any type of spending that could reduce its own receipts. Indeed, all groups loudly and continually press for a reduction in their own taxes and for increases in that part of government spending from which they benefit. Given these political biases it is not surprising that fiscal policy has erred toward the stimulative side. What is surprising is that the error has not been even larger.

Fiscal restraint is both difficult and unpopular. It has been invoked only twice in the past 20 years. One period was 1957-60, which was brought about by the mounting pressure of wage and price increases in 1956 and 1957. Richard Nixon, when he was President, found it hard to forget that period of restraint, for it had cost him the presidency in 1960. The second period of fiscal restraint began with the tax increase of 1968, which was invoked three years after we had embarked on a costly war and only after the rate of inflation had almost quadrupled. It did not last long. By 1970, while prices were still rising at 6 percent a year, the temptation to abandon the brake and step on the accelerator was already widespread.

All of the foregoing is history today. But in the final quarter of 1974, with inflation running at a rate in excess of 12 percent a year, both the antipathy toward the brake and the bias favoring the accelerator were apparent again. During the "Summit" meetings convened by President Ford in September 1974 to examine the inflation question, a significant body of opinion urged that the *real* problem was not whether or how to apply the brake, but how and when to reach for the accelerator.

3. **The problem of "uncontrollable" expenditures.** Fiscal restraint is hard to achieve for yet another reason. We have passed many laws without a careful projection of the long-run future costs of the programs created. Thus, huge annual increases in the level of government spending are now embedded in the system. As a result, some of the largest elements in total expenditure are now "uncontrollable" in the narrow budgeting sense—the future tilt toward greater spending on programs already incorporated in the budget can be reduced only by new legislation.

Federal *civilian* spending (total spending excluding defense and foreign aid) has risen extremely rapidly over the past 20 years. It was around $26 billion a year in fiscal year 1955 and is expected to exceed $230 billion in fiscal year 1975. The largest part of this total consists of transfer payments of various kinds—that is, payments made by the federal government which are *not* connected with the rendering of current services of any kind by their recipients (e.g., social security, unemployment, and welfare benefits). Such payments are extraordinarily difficult to hold down, let alone cut. To make matters worse many programs have automatic, built-in increases yet to come, and for some programs the potential growth of outlay could be extremely rapid. To cite just one example: The federal food stamp program was initiated in 1961; by 1965 some 400,000 persons received food stamps; by 1973 the number of recipients had risen to 12 million. It is now estimated that some 43 million persons will be eligible to participate in fiscal year 1975—although less than half of them are expected to do so.

The Structural Explanation

The socio-political factors we have just examined supplement rather than supplant the standard monetary explanation for inflation: Prices rise when there is an excess of total monetary demand relative to the total supply of goods and services. An excessive rise in the stock of money can be the factor which triggers the excess demand in the first place. Alternatively, the conditions of excess demand can be initiated by fiscal policy, which in turn leads to an excessive rise in the stock of money. In either case the pull of demand, backed by money, is the factor which starts prices rising and keeps them rising.

Many people, including some economists, are unhappy with the orthodox monetary explanation for inflation. They are even less happy with its implied prescription for curing inflation—or avoiding it in the first place. According to this group, modern inflation cannot be explained as a simple result of the *pull* of excessive *demand* fueled by excessive money creation; rather it is a new and different phenomenon which starts on the *cost* side of the economic equation. Rising costs, and especially rising wages, are supposed to *push* prices upward. The *cost-push* phenomenon itself is supposed to stem from *basic structural changes* which have developed in the modern U.S. economy. The notion of structural inflation is sufficiently widespread for it to warrant closer examination.

The cost-push or structural explanation for inflation runs along the following lines. The power of large unions and large corporations has grown to such an extent, they are able to set "administered" prices and wages; that is, prices and wage rates which are not responsive to basic market conditions of supply and demand. In this scenario, unions bargain for wage-rate increases in excess of gains in labor productivity, and the large corporations with whom they bargain grant such increases, knowing they can pass their increased costs on to the buyer in the form of higher prices. Neither group fears that it will "price" itself out of the market, because both have acquired virtual monopoly powers in their respective fields. The corporations cannot feasibly hire non-union labor, and the public has no adequate access to many products except from those corporations. Furthermore, both groups know that the national commitment to full employment will probably see to it that enough demand is eventually created to keep them both reasonably fully employed.

The behavior of wages in the construction industry is often cited as an extreme example of this kind of inflation. The year 1970 was a relatively poor one for the construction industry; building activity had fallen markedly, and between mid-1969 and mid-1970 the unemployment rate for construction workers had more than doubled from 5.5 percent to nearly 12 percent. Standard theory would suggest that the growing excess of labor supply relative to demand in this industry should bring wages down; in fact the opposite occurred. Construction workers, who had already received abnormally large wage increases in the late 1960s, accelerated their wage demands. During 1970, the more than 700,000 union workers who renegotiated wage settlements received wage and benefit increases that averaged nearly 20 percent in the first contract year. Much the same phenomenon occurred again in 1974. Between early 1973 and the summer of 1974 new housing starts fell by half and commercial construction had also weakened, yet wage rates in the construction industries accelerated rapidly.

Examples of large price increases by industry in the face of falling demand for its products can also be cited. In mid-1971 the U.S. steel industry was suffering from a relatively low level of demand for its output as well as increasing competition from steel imports and other substitutes—yet it attempted to *raise* prices by 12 percent. Similarly, the fact that the demand for automobiles in 1974 was running a full 25 percent lower than it had been a year earlier did not prevent car manufacturers from imposing huge increases on the price of new cars.

The essence of the structural explanation is that modern inflation is not caused by excessive demand but by the power of large corporations and unions to raise their prices and wage rates. Since one man's wage or one company's price is someone else's cost, the result is an interplay through which costs and prices are pushed upward through the exercise of market power.

The basic argument can be extended by citing ancillary structural developments which reinforce the inflationary effects of market power. One such argument is that the high wage increases granted to the organized goods-producing and transport sectors tend to spread to the growing service-producing sectors. The difference between the two sectors is that the inflationary effect of wage increases in the goods sector can be at least partly offset by productivity improvements through better capital equipment or more efficient work rules. Yet, for much of the pure service sector, the potential for productivity improvement is far smaller. At worst it may even be zero. (Two examples of zero productivity gain are the services of a baby-sitter and a live performance by a Haydn Quartet.) Thus, wage increases in service industries of the same magnitude as those occurring in the goods sector tend to be even more inflationary.

A second argument is that even in the sectors where potential gains in productivity are available, a change has taken place in worker attitudes which increasingly negates management's ability actually to extract such potential gains in man-hour output. For example, man-hour productivity in basic manufacturing industries such as steel, automobiles, and footwear showed virtually no improvement between 1968 and 1971. That poor performance was due partly to the sluggish overall level of activity in those industries, but many observers believe that it was also a result of a basic change in the work ethic of American workers. A sick joke about Detroit in those years was that it was unwise to buy a car assembled on a Friday because part of the regular assembly line team had left early for a long weekend; it was also unwise to buy one assembled on a Monday because part of the regular assembly line had not yet returned to work.

How valid are the structural arguments we have just outlined? Clearly they have some validity, and they do provide a partial explanation for some of the observed developments. The important question is whether structure as such and the cost-push phenomenon to which it leads are the major roots from which modern inflation springs, or, alternatively, whether the pull of excess demand is still the dominant root cause. The argument is important because it involves far more than the simple choice between two alternative theories.

Demand-Pull vs. Cost-Push

If the monetary or demand-pull factors provide the dominant explanation for inflation, two things follow: the "laws" of supply and demand are still working, and serious inflation can be prevented or corrected through traditional policy measures which work by preventing or curbing aggregate demand.

If on the other hand the structural factors provide the dominant explanation, it would suggest that in the future reasonably full employment and reasonable price stability cannot be simultaneously achieved within a free market economy. According to the structural view, modern inflation arises not because the laws of economics are working, but rather because they are not. In short, it implies that direct intervention or control over wage and price decisions must eventually become a permanent feature in the U.S. economy.

A Test of Two Theories

The decade of the 1960s provides an excellent test of the relative importance of the two alternative theories. By looking at just a few major variables, one can see that there was a remarkable contrast between the excellent performance of the U.S. economy during the first half of the decade and its poor performance during the second half.

From 1960 to 1965, output per man-hour in the private economy rose by 20 percent in five years—far better than our historic improvement in that measure of productivity. Compensation per man-hour rose by

22 percent, just about in line with productivity growth. Thus, unit labor costs in the whole private sector rose by less than 2 percent in five years. In the important manufacturing sector, unit labor costs actually fell. During this five-year period, the U.S. was a well-balanced, well-behaved economy relative both to its own past standards and to the other major economies of the world. Indeed, the performance of the U.S. economy was better than that achieved in virtually every other major economy. Our favorable performance and improving competitive edge both showed up clearly in our balance of trade in goods and services with the rest of the world. That balance, which was down to $1 billion in 1959, rose strongly to $6 billion in 1964 and in 1965. In mid-decade the only major fear expressed abroad about the U.S. economy was that it was, if anything, too competitive—as asserted, for example, in the widely cited book, *The American Challenge*, by Jean-Jacques Servan Schreiber.

After 1965 our economic performance changed rapidly. From 1965 to 1970, the productivity gain in the private sector was only 10 percent—about one-half the gain in the preceding five years. Furthermore, the annual rate of gain became increasingly worse as the decade progressed. Compensation per man-hour rose by nearly 40 percent, far in excess of the productivity gain, with the rate accelerating toward the end of the period. As a result, U.S. unit labor costs rose sharply—by 27 percent for the private economy as a whole and by almost as much in the manufacturing sector. In contrast, unit labor costs in Japan rose only 4 percent and not at all in Switzerland. In short, the U.S. was performing extremely badly—both in comparison with its own historic norms and relative to other major economies. France and the United Kingdom also experienced sharp increases in unit labor costs from 1965 to 1970, but because both currencies were devalued relative to the dollar, their unit labor costs *in terms of U.S. dollars* actually fell, thus making us *the worst* performer among the major economies.

The results of our deteriorating economic performance rapidly became apparent. Our competitive position, as measured by our balance of trade surplus, fell from +$6 billion a year to zero. In 1971 our balance of trade turned negative for the first time since 1893.

It is clear that long-term structural changes which have been going on for decades (such as the growing power of unions and corporations, the gradual shift from a goods-producing economy to a service-producing economy, or the alleged change in American work attitudes) cannot be the dominant explanation for the dramatic shift which took place in the behavior of wages, prices, and productivity after 1965. After all, we had the same corporations, the same unions, substantially the same leadership in both and substantially the same workers in 1965-70 as we had from 1960-65. Clearly the real reasons for the abrupt turn after 1965 must lie in developments which had their origin closer to that date. Those reasons are not hard to find.

In 1965, just as the U.S. economy was approaching the zone of full employment and an overall balance between aggregate demand and its aggregate capacity to supply, we embarked on two costly "wars." One war, undeclared, was Vietnam. Its cost rose swiftly to almost $30 billion dollars a year at its peak, and it went on for far longer than most people had envisioned in 1965. The second was the Great Society's declared war on poverty. Its cost also rose rapidly to almost $25 billion a year, and that cost has since become permanently embedded in our budget. Finally, tax rates were not increased to pay for either "war." The huge deficits which shortly developed were financed through the banking system, and led to a rapid increase in the money supply.

In more basic terms, both the "wars" on which we embarked required a major diversion of resources from the producing sector of the economy. Had that diversion been accomplished by an equivalent tax increase, aggregate demand would not have run ahead of aggregate supply, and we would not have generated the inflation which did follow. Instead, tax rates were not increased. The extra demand for the two wars was financed indirectly by creating more money.

The result was precisely what one would expect from a reading of chapter one of any "old-fashioned" book on monetary economics—a rapid acceleration in the rate of inflation, followed eventually by a devaluation of the dollar relative to better behaved currencies. The so-called "modern" changes in structure had little to do with that outcome.

Other episodes in our history tell much the same story: general inflation begins with the *demand* side of the equation, not with *costs* or *structure*. From 1897 to 1917, long before modern institutional cost-push factors were supposed to exist, wholesale prices more than doubled. From 1947 to 1967, with the so-called structural factors in full swing, wholesale prices rose only by about one-third.

The alleged power of unions and corporations does not lie in their ability to *push* up prices and wages at will. It lies rather in their ability to influence the overall political process, and through that process to influence the course of fiscal and monetary policies. Given the postwar expansionary bias in those policies, sufficient monetary demand is eventually created to restore overall full employment at the higher levels of wages, costs, and prices established by modern wage and price setting practices.

Price-Wage Interactions

The preceding sections have unabashedly supported the *demand* theory of the cause of inflation. What starts inflation is excess demand, fed by, or accompanied by, excessive increases in the supply of money. Without the pull of monetary demand, prices in general will not start a rapid rise. Without the continued pressure from demand-pull, such rises as do occur cannot be sustained for long.

However, while the structural or cost-push explanation for inflation is wrong insofar as the *cause* of inflation is concerned, it does have a major influence on the *course* of inflation once the process begins. Indeed, the interaction of costs and prices is an important reason for the continuation of inflationary behavior in modern societies, even after the original cause itself is removed.

As in many other aspects of human life, the *cause* and *cure* of inflation are not symmetrical. For example, a person develops amoebic dysentery because he drinks contaminated water; but the disease, once contracted, does not go away just by switching to good water. Clearly, a *necessary* or essential condition for an enduring cure is to stop drinking more contaminated water; but that is not in itself a *sufficient* condition for a rapid cure. Once contracted, the disease develops a life of its own. So it is with inflation.

The process of inflationary interaction goes as follows. A rise in the price level, originally caused by excessive monetary demand, reduces the relative income share of many groups in society—including the share of many large corporations and unions. When the opportunity arises, those groups quite naturally attempt to restore their relative positions through wage and price increases. So long as the level of total demand is high, the process of "catch-up" increases in wages, prices, and fees spreads to still other sectors of the economy. In the process, the general level of prices keeps moving upward.

There are several structural factors in today's economy which tend to speed the upward process of wage-price interaction. The important factors are *not* the ones usually mentioned.

One significant factor is the change which has taken place in the attitude of groups sometimes referred to as the bourgeoisie. In the past those groups—which are roughly comprised of salaried workers, including government employees, and school teachers—were generally willing to accept a relative loss in their real incomes during periods of rapid wage and price increases. That willingness, which served to dampen the upward spiral, is now a thing of the past. Increasingly, members have learned to organize, unionize, and strike or otherwise bargain in order to maintain or improve their real incomes. A related development is the practice of granting annual wage increases to individuals in the non-unionized groups (such as clerical workers) not on the basis of bilateral bargains but on the basis of whatever *general pattern* prevails in a given town or country. Indeed, regular surveys are conducted for that purpose.

The effect of both changes is that we now get a broader and much more rapid diffusion of wage increases than used to be the case. As a result, once a marked rise in prices and wages occurs in one or more conspicuous sectors, the rise tends to generate a bigger overall rise in the wage-price level than was the case 20 years ago.

The modern system of tax-and-transfer payments has brought about yet another major change in the response of wage rates to inflation. A progressive income tax system, and especially one which is collected largely on a pay-as-you-go basis, erodes the purchasing power of after-tax income even when wages rise as rapidly as prices in general. This fact tends to increase the pressure for even higher money wages. At the same time, we now have a generous system of unemployment benefits and other benefits (some of which are tax-free) which reduce the net financial cost of being out of work and therefore increase the willingness and ability of workers to hold out for larger wage gains than they might otherwise seek.

None of the structural factors is in itself a primary cause of inflation, but all of them serve to increase the momentum and hence the duration of inflation once the process begins. It took just about a year to unwind the sharp spurt of inflation caused by the creation of excess demand during the Korean War. The swell of excess demand created by the Vietnam War took longer to break out into inflation, but it is now proving to be a far more intractable spiral than any we have experienced before. The duration and severity of the post-Vietnam inflation is worse than the inflation after the Korean War for many reasons.

The initiating cause of the current inflation was itself a more powerful one. In addition, modern structural factors have clearly accelerated the course of inflation. Finally, we have been the victims of extraordinary events since 1970, especially in the international markets. Those events have had a powerful influence on the behavior of U.S. prices. Indeed, the wave of inflation we experienced in 1973 and 1974 was triggered largely by international rather than purely domestic interactions. We turn now to a discussion of those influences.

Drawing by Tony Auth
Courtesy *Philadelphia Inquirer*

CHAPTER THREE

INTERNATIONAL MONETARY CONFUSION

THE FEVER OF INFLATION initially set off by four years of policy excesses, 1965 to 1968, did not run the course which that disease typically follows after its primary cause is removed. Instead we have had one complication after another—many of them international in scope. Some of these complications can be related within a discernible sequence of events, but some were random. Their combined effect propelled us into a secondary wave of inflation in 1974 which was twice as high as the primary wave we experienced in 1969 and 1970.

Few periods in our peacetime history can match the barrage of upsetting international economic events we have experienced since 1970. Four developments in particular had a significant effect on the level of prices. Two of these developments are discussed in the present chapter:

1. The huge increase in the world's money supply that was fostered by the then-prevailing system of fixed exchange rates.
2. The devaluation of the U.S. dollar, in 1971 and 1973.

The two other international developments which had a major effect on the course of inflation (discussed in the following chapters) were:

1. The worldwide crop failures of 1972.
2. The oil embargo and the quadrupling of oil prices in late 1973 and early 1974.

The Fixed Exchange Rate System: Bretton Woods

In order to appreciate the effect which a system of fixed exchange rates had on the acceleration of inflation after 1971, we have to undertake a minor diversion to understand the system itself.

Between 1946 and 1971 the free world operated under an international monetary system known as "Bretton Woods." A key element in this system was that each major nation set and maintained a *par* value of exchange for its currency. A nation was allowed to alter its currency's established par value, but the presumption was that such alterations would be infrequent and that they would be invoked only after consultation with, and the approval of, other major nations.

Each country was required to maintain its currency's par value of exchange in one of two ways—either relative to gold or to a key currency which itself maintained its par value of exchange relative to gold. Only the United States was in a position to adopt the first approach; we elected to do so. This decision meant we were willing to accept U.S. dollars tendered by foreign central banks or international organizations such as the International Monetary Fund (IMF) and to pay them gold at $35 per ounce. Alternatively, we undertook to accept gold tendered by them and to pay them dollars at that rate.

All of the other nations which observed the par value rule elected to do so by pegging their currencies to the U.S. dollar. Each central bank agreed to maintain the external value of its currency within a narrow band of plus or minus 1 percent around its par value, by using U.S. dollars to buy its own currency (when that currency declined to 1 percent below its par value) or by using its own currency to buy and hold U.S. dollars (when that currency rose to 1 percent above its par value). A few of the weaker economies, mainly in South America, were exempted from the par value requirement and were allowed to let their exchange rates drift downward relative to the dollar more or less continuously.

As far as the major nations were concerned, we in effect had a system of fixed exchange rates tied to the U.S. dollar. Gradually the U.S. dollar became the key currency of the free world—its principal unit of account, its principal form of international reserve money, and indeed its principal medium of exchange for international transactions.

The system worked reasonably well so long as the dollar maintained its status as a stable, desirable currency. The status of the dollar in turn depended crucially on the status of the U.S. itself as a strong, stable, and competitive economy, which for over 75 years had consistently required less in the way of imports from the rest of the world than the rest of the world had required from it.

From time to time one or more of the major non-U.S. currencies, such as the British pound or the French franc, would go through a period of serious weakness. That weakness might be caused by domestic inflation, low productivity (due to strikes, crop failures, or other factors), or extraordinary overseas spending (such as the French war in Algeria). Whatever the reason, it would show up in the foreign exchange market as follows: some outsiders receiving that nation's currency would try to exchange it for dollars rather than hold it or use it for other purposes. To maintain the par value of its currency the Bank of France or the Bank of England would therefore have to buy the francs or pounds that were being turned in, using dollar reserves for that purpose. Since their dollar holdings were limited, basic corrective action also had to be taken to stop the outflow of reserves.

Two forms of corrective action were available. The nation suffering an outflow of reserves, an international deficit, could "tighten its belt." It did so by taking steps to lower its rate of growth, reduce its rate of inflation, or reduce the net outflow of its currency to the rest of the world in yet other ways, such as import controls. It could also take steps to increase its domestic interest rates relative to rates elsewhere, and thereby increase the inflow of funds *from* the rest of the world. If balance could not be restored rapidly enough by those actions, the nation suffering a deficit could *devalue* its currency, i.e., reduce its official par value relative to the dollar.

Devaluation corrects the underlying imbalance in two ways. It stops speculation against the currency and thereby reduces some of the existing pressure to convert that currency into dollars. It also improves the relative competitive position of domestic products and so leads to a rise in exports relative to imports, which in turn reduces the deficit and hence the potential demand for currency conversion.

Under the Bretton Woods system, inflation in any one country (except the United States) caused or accompanied by an undue expansion in its money supply had only a *limited* effect on other countries. The inflating country would suck in imports from other economies, which would be stimulative to those economies, but only for a while. Outsiders would quickly find themselves holding an excess supply of the inflating country's currency and would soon thereafter turn in that supply for dollars or some other preferred currency. The inflating currency would then have to take steps either to curb its inflationary behavior or to devalue.

To take an extreme example, the Republic of Chile has had the habit of expanding its money supply at an extraordinary rate. However, the flood of Chilean escudos has not caused any inflation outside of Chile. All that happens, internationally, is that the exchange value of the escudo falls as fast as, or faster than, domestic Chilean prices rise.

But what happens within a system of fixed exchange rates when the key currency country—the United States—is the one that is "inflating"? What happens when the key currency itself becomes available to the rest of the world in excess amounts? The answer is quite different. In a system of fixed exchange rates, a flood of U.S. dollars does tend to generate a flood of monetary creation throughout the world. The increase in the global money supply in turn becomes a major cause of worldwide inflation, which, like an echo, returns to push U.S. prices to even higher levels. Why this scenario became an actuality after 1970 is now explained.

Fixed Exchange Rates and Inflation

Between 1965 and 1970 U.S. imports grew much more rapidly than U.S. exports. This situation occurred for two major reasons. As we saw earlier, U.S. costs and prices, measured in terms of U.S. dollars, rose faster between 1965 and 1971 than costs and prices in any other major economy. In the process, U.S. goods and services became less competitive with respect to foreign goods and services, both in this country and abroad. In addition the U.S. was at war in Vietnam, and the other major nations were not. As a result, our capacity to serve combined civilian and military needs was strained. Our need and ability to expand exports diminished, while our dependence on imports—including the indirect imports required to service half a million troops in Southeast Asia—increased.

The growing net availability of foreign goods and services was initially counter-inflationary, for they absorbed part of the excess demand generated during the buildup of the potentially inflationary boom we had instigated. Also, at the fixed exchange rates which then prevailed, foreign goods and services, on average, were priced lower than domestic goods.

Foreign nations, faced with the prospect of rising surpluses in their transactions with the U.S., had two alternatives. They could have let the excess supply of dollars pile up in their foreign exchange markets, which would have led to a fall in the value of the dollar relative to most other currencies. Instead, the central banks of the principal surplus nations supported the exchange value of the dollar whenever it sank below its established par value. They did so by purchasing dollars in exchange for their own currency, sometimes in large amounts. Technically speaking, they were simply carrying out the intent of the Bretton Woods system—keeping the value of their own currency within plus or minus 1 percent of its par value relative to the U.S. dollar. In fact, they were probably pursuing other objectives.

Japan provides a good illustration of what happened, although this same analysis could be applied equally to most of the continental European countries. At the fixed exchange rate of 360 yen to the dollar, which was maintained through 1971, the yen had become seriously undervalued relative to the U.S. dollar. (Alternatively, we can say the U.S. dollar had become seriously overvalued with respect to the Japanese yen.) The degree of dollar overvaluation increased rapidly during the period from 1965 to 1971.

From the point of view of Japanese society as a whole, the undervaluation of the yen was neither demonstrably good nor bad. That neutrality did not apply to particular segments of Japanese society. By and large, Japanese *consumers* were hurt because they paid more for goods imported from the U.S.; their yen was worth less abroad when they traveled as tourists or when, as investors, they purchased land and securities. In the final analysis, a policy which kept the exchange value of the yen below its true value caused Japanese consumers to give up more goods and services to U.S. residents (including U.S. tourists to Japan and U.S. investors in Japanese industry) than the volume of goods and services they received from U.S. residents.

Why then did the Japanese government persist in holding up the exchange value of the U.S. dollar? It did so because the picture is quite different when it is viewed through the eyes of the Japanese people as *producers*. The artificially low exchange value of the yen gave Japanese producers (which includes both industry and labor) distinct advantages: Their output would be more competitive, both at home and abroad; sales and employment would expand; profits and wages would rise.

Prior to December 1971 the Japanese government, consciously or otherwise, must have decided that yen undervaluation provided greater overall benefits than costs. That decision may have been influenced by several considerations:

1. The greater overall political voice the Japanese people had in their capacity as producers, relative to their voice as consumers or investors.
2. The national policy emphasis on fast growth of industry and industrial employment.
3. A national need to build their stock of international reserves.

In any case, the national policy option selected was for the Japanese Central Bank to pay out yen to support the dollar at close to the fixed

360 to 1 rate. As the inflow of dollars kept growing, the objective of holding up its value at the official 360 to 1 rate became increasingly inflationary. Each time the Japanese Central Bank bought a U.S. dollar to maintain its official value against the yen, it pushed more yen into circulation in Japan.

It was thus that the rising U.S. deficit, which started in the first place because of our own internal fiscal and monetary expansion, became an engine of inflation for Japan. Our large and growing demand for their goods and services was in itself a minor cause of inflation in Japan. A far more important cause was their internal monetary expansion, which occurred because the Japanese Central Bank kept on creating yen, to buy an increasing flood of dollars, in order to hold the yen/dollar rate at the fixed but incorrect level of 360 to 1.

What happened in Japan happened also in Germany, the Netherlands, and a dozen other coutries.

U.S. Policies To Curb the Dollar Outflow

The U.S. did take a number of steps to curb the outflow of dollars and to correct the deficit which was causing the outflow. We tried to hold down the outflow of capital funds by imposing various controls on the rights of U.S. citizens and corporations to lend and invest abroad. We tried to minimize the deficit caused by U.S. governmental grants and loans by insisting that recipients spend a substantial part of those proceeds in the U.S. We tried to minimize the net foreign exchange cost of our military operations abroad by having our own armed forces and some allies "Buy American" even when purchases could have been made abroad more cheaply. But, at best, all of those little steps merely prevented the deficit from worsening more rapidly than it did. For example, despite such efforts, the net foreign exchange cost of our military operations alone still drained well over $3-billion a year, and U.S. investments abroad kept rising.

A second set of policies is also available to a nation suffering an international deficit: The nation can slow its own rate of expansion. The U.S. adopted such a policy at the end of 1968. Tax rates were raised, monetary policy was tightened, and the long rise in manpower devoted to defense was halted and then sharply reversed. The restoration of balance in our international payments was not the only motive for these policy actions, but it was one of the major considerations.

A counter-inflationary policy helps to cure an international deficit in several ways. The domestic demand for foreign goods and services declines with the slowing growth of economic activity and incomes. Domestic industry buys fewer goods from abroad when a margin of excess capacity develops at home; consumers import less when their incomes stop rising; and tourists spend less on overseas travel. At the same time, domestic industry, spurred by a rise in excess productive capacity, increases its selling efforts in overseas markets.

A counter-inflationary policy also works because it affects the behavior of prices in the domestic economy relative to foreign prices. When domestic prices fall, or rise at a slower rate than foreign prices, the competitive position of U.S. producers improves, both at home and abroad. Exports rise faster than imports, which reduces or reverses the dollar outflow.

The effect of a counter-inflationary policy on interest rates also serves to reduce or reverse the net dollar outflow. As restrictive monetary policy raises domestic interest rates relative to rates abroad, it thus reduces the outflow of U.S. funds seeking investment abroad and induces an inflow of investment funds into the domestic financial market.

The policies adopted by the U.S. in 1969 and 1970 did produce favorable results. The net outflow of dollars to foreign central banks stopped and turned into a net inflow in 1969. The flow reversed itself again in 1970, but confidence in the U.S. dollar remained reasonably high for several reasons:

1. We had demonstrated our willingness and ability to end the highly inflationary policies of the 1965-68 period.
2. There were tangible moves toward disengagement in Vietnam, including a reduction in our military forces stationed there.
3. Our basic merchandise trade balance improved by about $2 billion a year in 1970.
4. The net outflow of dollars to foreign central banks which began again in 1970 was not regarded then as serious because many of these central banks (notably West Germany's) had lost dollar reserves in 1969, and they were not unhappy to see their reserve positions increase.

The relatively placid attitudes of 1970 did not last long. The restrictive policies adopted in the U.S. grew onerous in 1970. Tight money and high interest rates depressed the housing industry and constricted the financial markets. The Penn-Central Railroad failed. Common stock prices fell sharply. Unemployment rose rapidly to the 6 percent level, mainly because the economy was in a recession but also because of the rapid reduction in the volume of defense-related employment, including the armed forces. Thus despite our rate of inflation, which was still high by past standards, and despite our international position, which was still extremely weak, the counter-inflationary U.S. policy emphasis was switched in midstream in order to get the economy expanding again.

In Europe, and especially in West Germany, the original shift to a deflationary policy of monetary restraint began later than it had in the U.S., but it was maintained longer. With the tightening of West German monetary policy and the concurrent easing of U.S. monetary policy, U.S. interest rates declined relative to rates in Germany. At this time, the West German economy was already in an exceptionally strong position internationally because it had a huge and growing surplus of trade. This economic strength, combined with the attractive interest rates available in the German market, kicked off a renewed outflow of U.S. dollars in 1970, mainly to Germany. By early 1971 it looked as if that outflow would grow into an avalanche. It did. Something had to "give"; the question was, what? The U.S. faced a dilemma, as did West Germany (along with the other strong currencies of Europe, such as the Swiss franc, the Dutch guilder, the Austrian schilling, and the Belgian franc). The individual national dilemmas were by no means alike, but all had one prong in common—that was the Bretton Woods system of fixed-exchange rates. Eventually that was the prong which "gave."

The really difficult problems of economic policy are those that require democratically determined solutions to national dilemmas. Deep down, those issues frequently turn out to be political rather than economic. It is useful for two reasons to examine the international monetary dilemmas faced by the U.S. and Europe in 1971. They illustrate the way in which policy dilemmas emerge, and they provide one of those heartening instances in which the eventual resolution of an economic dilemma follows the path indicated by academic economists.

The Devaluation of the U.S. Dollar

The resumption of large dollar outflows in 1970 had a clear meaning. At the old fixed rates of exchange, the U.S. dollar was fundamentally out of line with the other major currencies. This imbalance could not be corrected by the package of minor control measures adopted prior to 1968, nor could it be corrected by the relatively short and mild switch to deflation attempted in 1969 and 1970. Nor was the U.S. willing to tolerate the pain of a longer and deeper slump in its domestic economy. The logical cure for the monetary imbalance was a downward change in the exchange value of the dollar. Any other nation would either have voluntarily adopted that measure by devaluing or else it would have been forced, by other nations, to devalue. But the U.S. was in a unique position within the Bretton Woods family.

"WHY CAN'T YOU JUST FLOAT LIKE THE REST OF US?"

For every other nation, the existence of a fundamental imbalance in the external value of its currency would show up quite rapidly. For example, if the French franc is overvalued with respect to other currencies, there would be an excessive outflow of francs to foreigners. Those excess francs would be presented in the foreign exchange market in Paris for conversion into more desired currencies. The exchange value of the franc would fall. The Central Bank of France would use its stock of reserves (principally U.S. dollars) to buy francs in order to prop up its exchange value. When its stock of dollars appeared to be running out, France might try to borrow more from other governments, through special arrangements. If the outflow of francs continues, some of those precious borrowed dollars would also have to be spent in order to keep propping up the franc's value.

Beyond this point the scenario runs a fairly set course. The government of France would issue pious bulletins assuring people that the franc was *not* going to be devalued. The purpose of the bulletins would be to prevent an even greater outflow of francs by speculators who anticipate a devaluation and hence see the possibility of a high rate of profit to be derived by borrowing francs in Paris, exchanging those francs for dollars at the old fixed rate, and later reconverting the dollars into francs after the expected devaluation does in fact occur.

The size of the speculative profits to be made if one anticipates devaluation correctly can be very high. For example, assume that I correctly anticipate that the franc is going to be devalued by around 20-30 percent within 30 days. I put up 100,000 francs of my own and borrow 1,000,000 francs from my bank at 12 percent interest a year, or 1 percent a month. I use my 1,100,000 francs to buy dollars. If the exchange rate is 4 Fr = 1 dollar, I get 275,000 dollars. I hold those dollars in a bank at 6 percent annual interest or $\frac{1}{2}$ percent a month. The franc is devalued to 5 Fr = 1 dollar within the week. I convert my dollars back to francs, receiving 1,375,000 francs.

I have to pay a week's interest at 12 percent and some transaction costs. But I receive a week's interest at 6 percent. The net transaction cost is trivial—perhaps 2,000 francs, and certainly no more than 5,000 francs including the cost of telephone calls and several dinners. But I now have 1,370,000 francs. I pay off my 1,000,000 franc debt to the bank and am left with 370,000 francs. I started with only 100,000 francs. My net gain amounts to 270 percent *a week*. The annualized rate of gain is staggering. I am also a hero to my family, and I have enjoyed several excellent dinners to boot.

When a currency is "at bay," the speculative flows run hard. Therefore soon after the French minister of finance announces that the franc will not be devalued, it *is* in fact devalued, generally over a weekend; hence the saying, "He lied like a finance minister on the eve of devaluation."

When the U.S. dollar was the currency in fundamental imbalance the scenario was a different one. Parties who received the outflow of dollars did not present them to the foreign exchange market in New York for conversion into other currencies. They presented the dollars to their own exchange markets—in Paris or Tokyo or Frankfurt, for example. When the value of the excess dollars declined in foreign markets, the Federal Reserve System (our Central Bank) did not intervene by selling international reserves held in the form of marks or yen or francs to prop up the dollar's exchange value. We did not even hold our reserves in those forms; we held our reserves mainly in gold. The next move was entirely up to the French, the Germans, and the Japanese. They chose to prop up the exchange value of the dollar by buying it from their citizens at its fixed value. This action created the dilemma.

The European Dilemma

As the dollars kept flowing into Europe, their central banks, especially the West German Central Bank (to which most of the dollars flowed), found themselves in a dilemma. The dilemma, or trilemma if one insists on being a purist, had three horns.

1. West Germany was pursuing a policy of credit restraint in order to combat inflation, a disease that causes almost as much national anxiety among politicians in Germany as unemployment does among politicians in the United States. One necessary element in that policy was that the Central Bank should *not* be creating more deutschemarks by buying financial assets (such as dollars) from the public. (Every time any central bank buys any asset it actually *creates* money.)

2. Yet, in order to maintain the value of the dollar—which it also wanted to do—Germany was forced to keep buying the U.S. dollars presented to it, thereby creating more deutschemarks than its policy of monetary restraint was willing to tolerate.

3. West Germany *could* have imposed a rigid system of exchange-control regulations, stipulating, for example, that nationals could not borrow dollars abroad and that German exporters or hotel-keepers who received dollars through legitimate trade would have to report in quintuplicate exactly how and when they received those dollars. But because of their experience with exchange controls during the Hitler regime, the West Germans loathe exchange controls almost as much as they fear inflation.

By May 1971, West Germany faced the prospect of adopting at least one of three unpleasant alternatives: It could keep swallowing the inflow of dollars by buying them at the old fixed rate of 3.77 marks to one dollar; it could *revalue* the mark upward and so end the inflow of excess dollars; it could stop supporting the dollar and thereby let the value of the mark *float* upward.

The first alternative was unpleasant because it would lead to the creation of more marks than Germany's counter-inflationary policy was willing to tolerate. The second alternative would have been politically unpopular. Like their Japanese counterparts, the German export industries liked the undervalued mark. It kept foreign prices of their products cheap and thus enabled them to sell more abroad. Any government which deliberately raised the external value of the mark when it didn't legally have to do so would have become quite unpopular with the politically important export industries. It also would have antagonized German farmers. The European Common Market had a strange arrangement for subsidizing farmers—the subsidies payable under the agreement were stipulated in U.S. dollars. Revaluing the mark upward would reduce the value of the subsidy payments to German farmers, which were of course made in marks.

The third alternative—allowing the value of the German mark to float upward in the marketplace would bypass the disadvantage of the two other alternatives. But it would signal the breakdown of the Bretton Woods system of fixed exchange rates.

An additional difficulty was present. There was no way in which West Germany could revalue *only* against the dollar. Other governments, such as France, which were faced with much smaller pressures of dollar inflows, might have held their currencies at the old fixed rates. All of which meant the deutschemark would rise in relative value not just against the dollar but also against the franc, the lira, and a host of other currencies. That the West Germans were not prepared to do. During 1968 and 1969, after France devalued during its troubles, the exchange value of the mark relative to the franc had been raised by over 20 percent. Because France was Germany's largest trading partner, Germany was not anxious to let the mark-franc rate get even higher.

The U.S. Dilemma

The U.S. could have relieved the German dilemma through taking action to correct the overvaluation of the dollar by devaluing. But the U.S., too, was faced with intractable problems.

In the first place, governments of large nations do not like the onus of devaluation on their records. In countries with parliamentary systems of government it was fairly common at that time for finance ministers to resign when events eventually forced them to devalue the nation's currency.

More importantly, when Congress ratified the Bretton Woods Agreement in 1945, it also legislated that the U.S. President had to obtain Congressional authority before proposing or agreeing to any change in the par value of the dollar. Any such proposal, in the context of 1971, would have announced an impending dollar devaluation. Such an announcement would have led to a predictable avalanche of speculative outflows.

Finally, there was no assurance at all that the majority of the world's nations would have *allowed* the U.S. to achieve an effective devaluation against their currencies. The U.S. could have devalued against gold, but other nations could have followed us down by devaluing their currencies to the same extent. Nothing would have been solved as far as exchange rates were concerned. All we would have had is an increase in the official price of gold. The government of France let it be known, more than once, that they would not have been unhappy to see just that scenario occur.

What was needed was a formal international meeting of all of the key nations for the purpose of realigning the entire set of fixed exchange rates among them. Alternatively, the key currencies could have agreed to abandon the system of fixed rates in favor of a *floating* system in which currencies would be allowed to seek their own true exchange-values in the marketplace, without any artificial central bank intervention. Academic opinion, in and out of the various governments, favored such a move. But almost everybody else, including the private sector and the bulk of official opinion in finance ministries and central banks, opposed the idea.

Meanwhile the flow of dollars kept growing, and events overtook the policy makers. On May 5, 1971, the flood of dollars flowing into the German Central Bank reached the staggering rate of $1 billion *an hour*. The Central Bank stopped buying and let the dollar value of the mark rise. The flow of speculation moved to other "strong currencies." The Netherlands and, soon after, Belgium (which had two rates, one fixed and one free) followed Germany's example. Switzerland and Austria responded in more orthodox fashion and revalued their official rates upward. By June it was becoming clear that the problem was not that one or two currencies were strong, but that the U.S. dollar was fundamentally weak.

Why didn't the central banks which were taking in all those dollars present them to the U.S. Treasury for conversion into gold? Some did, but by and large everybody was restrained by the knowledge that such a move would be self-defeating. The U.S. stock of reserve assets, mainly gold, was only around $14 billion—far smaller than the total stock of dollars held by central banks abroad. In the summer of that year, there were renewed pressures by the private sector to convert dollars into foreign currencies, which kicked off additional pressures by foreign central banks to convert part of the dollars they were accumulating into U.S. gold. In the best tradition of finance ministers, the U.S. Secretary of the Treasury announced that the dollar would not be devalued, which increased the conviction that it would. The flood began again. On August 15, 1971, the President of the U.S. announced that we were suspending the convertibility of the dollar into anything else. The dollar's value relative to most of the world's principal currencies started to move down. Bretton Woods was dead. But the world was not ready then to move to a "floating" system.

The Smithsonian Agreement

In December 1971, after a preliminary meeting with the French President, the President of the U.S. convened a meeting of the free world's principal financial nations at the Smithsonian Institution in Washington. There it was agreed that the U.S. would acknowledge its own contribution to the situation by officially devaluing the dollar relative to gold by 7.89 percent. (The official price of gold was raised from $35 a troy ounce to $38, subject, of course, to Congressional approval.) This dollar devaluation with respect to gold gave the U.S. dollar an effective devaluation of about the same percentage against France, the United Kingdom, Italy and Sweden. At the same time Japan, West Germany, the Netherlands, and Belgium raised their currency values relative to gold, thus giving the U.S. dollar an even larger devaluation with respect to those currencies.

The Smithsonian agreement was a last-ditch attempt to salvage a system of fixed rates. But it did not last for long. Viable exchange rates probably cannot be set by computerized calculations. They certainly cannot be set by political bargains, which apparently is what happened at the Smithsonian meetings.

In just over a year it became clear that the structure of semi-fixed exchange rates set in December 1971 was not going to be a lasting one. The United Kingdom pound had been set too high, and by June 1972 it was devalued and allowed to "float" (i.e., nobody tried to support its exchange value at any fixed rate). In January 1973, there was a large outflow of lire from Italy, principally to Switzerland, and the lira was allowed to float. To gain greater control over their own monetary policy the Swiss allowed their franc to float. That move, by a country noted for its financial orthodoxy, led to widespread expectations that the system of fixed exchange rates was coming to a final end. It was. In February the U.S. dollar was devalued again, by 10 percent, without any of the usual fuss or bother. Furthermore, the U.S. announced that it would be quite happy to let the new value of the dollar float to whatever level the market dictated. The same day the Japanese government announced that the yen would be allowed to float upward. The Bretton Woods system which had died in August 1971 was buried in February 1973. Since that time we have been in a system of floating exchange rates.

Devaluation and U.S. Inflation

The long process of devaluation, from 1970 to 1973, had several large effects on U.S. inflation. In the process, world holdings of international reserves doubled from around $80 billion to $160 billion. Most of this reflected the outflow of U.S. dollars absorbed by foreign central banks. Every such absorption created money in the absorbing nations. As a result the world's money supply also grew extremely rapidly.

This rise in the world's stock of money generated, and in late 1974 was still generating, worldwide inflation. Prices of goods and services will rise until all of the excess liquidity we created is absorbed.

The devaluation of the dollar had a particular effect on the behavior of prices in the principal devaluing country—namely us. As inflation progressed, it led to a quantum jump in the world price of many basic staples such as food and feed grains, petroleum, lumber, metals, and paper. Because the value of the devalued dollar was lower than it had been, prices jumped even more in terms of dollars. For example, if the price of wheat or oil rises by 100 percent in terms of West German marks, and the mark itself is up by 50 percent relative to the dollar, then the price of wheat or oil expressed in U.S. dollars (which is the only way we see it) must be up by 200 percent. Finally, if devaluation does serve its original purpose, which is to increase the U.S. price of imported goods and to increase the foreign demand for U.S. goods, that in itself places upward pressures on the U.S. price level.

Thus it was that the devaluation of the dollar, which was itself originally brought about by the inflation we engaged in from 1965 to 1968, later became a cause of the inflation we suffered in 1973 and 1974.

Courtesy Personality Posters, Inc.

CHAPTER FOUR

THE EXPERIMENT WITH CONTROLS: 1971-1974

SUSPENSION OF THE DOLLAR'S CONVERTIBILITY on August 15, 1971, was not the only major policy action taken on that date. In the same speech, the President announced the immediate imposition of a 90-day freeze on wages, prices, and rents to be followed by an unspecified period of mandated controls over future changes in these items. He also asked Congress to enact a number of tax cuts as soon as possible as part of a shift to a more expansionary fiscal policy.

We will probably never know for certain how each person involved in that decisive turn of policy first arrived at the conclusion that something had to be done. But we can review the ideas that eventually culminated in the three-part policy package. Such a review is useful for two reasons:

1. It may help to explain why we are where we are now.
2. It will illustrate the policy dilemmas which mixed economies like our own face from time to time. This is important because what we faced in 1971 may well face us again in 1975, and on an even larger scale.

Three Problems

One constant the public can always count on in matters of economic policy is that there will be more than one point of view. In mid-1971 the room for controversy was especially large. The economy was confronted by not just one problem but three, each of which was somehow connected to the other two.

The dollar. For some people the crucial problem which required action in 1971 was the rapid deterioration of the dollar's external exchange value. The policy options ranged all the way from "do nothing," at one extreme, to talk of direct exchange controls over imports and exports, including the idea of trading blocs, at the other. The rationale for doing nothing was so well thought through it even had a name—"benign neglect." The concept was simple enough. If the rest of world officialdom kept buying U.S. dollars it was because they wanted to do so. If they didn't want to buy, they could stop doing so and let the value of the dollar float (in this instance, a euphemism for "sink"). As we saw in Chapter Three, the world is more complex than this rationale allows. Any one nation which permitted the exchange value of the dollar to sink against its own currency faced the prospect that the exchange value of its own currency would rise, not just against the dollar but against every other currency in the world. Few countries were prepared to face that outcome.

The option at the other end of the spectrum didn't have a name, but it did have a small following. Some people toyed with the idea of correcting the outflow of U.S. dollars by imposing a system of direct controls over most trade and investment transactions requiring foreign exchange. These controls would include import quotas, special tariffs, regional trading blocs, and similar devices. The persons who invented the phrase "benign neglect" might have called this latter approach a policy of "malevolent intervention."

Most economists, however, believed that some form of exchange rate devaluation was both inevitable and correct, that the marketplace was the best and fairest guide to a new set of equilibrium rates, and that formal devaluation was a way station to a more flexible system of exchange rates. This solution was the one eventually selected.

But devaluation, in itself, would achieve no lasting correction unless the inflation causing the erosion of the dollar's exchange value was also removed at the same time. Thus, the need to devalue in 1971 led also to the need for measures to curb future inflationary behavior in the U.S. economy. During 1969 and 1970 the U.S. had already tried all of the standard steps available for curbing inflation. The question in 1971 was what else should be done?

Expansion and productivity. For some people, the switch to fiscal activism in mid-1971 was motivated by the need to push the U.S. economy onto a more expansionary track than it was then enjoying. That need for faster expansion was not simply a matter of combating the 6 percent rate of unemployment which had prevailed all through the first half of 1971. It had a subtler logic as well:

1. The persistence of inflationary behavior in mid-1971 was not due to the persistence of excess demand. Excess demand had been eliminated.

2. Workers were demanding higher wages and companies were demanding higher prices because both groups felt deprived of any genuine increases during the preceding few years, and indeed they had been.

3. A substantial increase in productivity is the only way in which labor and capital can simultaneously achieve increases both in *real* income per unit of work and *real* income per unit of investment. If that increase in productivity could be achieved it would slow, or even halt, the ongoing grab for higher wages and prices for which both individual labor unions and corporations were scrambling in order to rectify the perceived losses they had suffered in the preceding period.

4. In the U.S. economy, it is relatively easy and pleasant for policy to bring about a substantial increase in productivity by taking steps to expand the level of total output rapidly without a corresponding increase in the level of employment. By contrast, it is extremely difficult and unpleasant to achieve gains in productivity by laying off workers.

5. But total output cannot grow unless total demand is expanding. This brings us to the prescription for mid-1971: Expand the economy by taking steps to expand *demand*; this would increase *output*, which in turn would increase *productivity*, which would allow both *real wages* and *returns on capital* to rise. These tangible gains would bring a halt to the grabby behavior of individual unions and companies which was causing the hangover of inflation we had in mid-1971.

The steps taken to expand total demand in mid-1971 included tax cuts, higher government spending, and an easier monetary policy. However, a stimulative policy which created a net increase in aggregate demand would not achieve its ultimate objective if that increased demand were allowed either to leak out through larger imports and balance of payments deficits or to expend its force merely inflating the level of domestic prices and wages. Thus, to achieve the ultimate desired results, it was also necessary to take action to minimize those two potential leakages. The need to protect against such leakage of demand explains why people who believed that a switch to a faster economic track was the crucial issue in mid-1971 also felt that such a switch had to be accompanied by at least temporary curbs on wage and price increases and on dollar outflows.

Price and wage controls. To yet another group of people, the central problem in mid-1971 was perceived to be the continued manifestation of inflationary behavior long after the pressure of excess demand had been removed. Although the overall rate of increase in consumer prices had abated significantly from 6.1 percent in 1969 to below 3 percent during the first quarter of 1971, there were clear signs of a resurgence of inflationary behavior in the second quarter of that year. For example, if the effects of fluctuations in food prices and mortgage interest rates are removed from the Consumer Price Index, prices in other sectors of the economy increased more rapidly during the spring quarter of 1971 (6.2 percent a year) than they had risen in either 1969 (5.2 percent) or 1970 (5.9 percent). In the spring of 1971, wholesale industrial prices, which provide a revealing preview of future changes in non-food prices, also rose faster than they had risen at the peak of the preceding inflation.

The resurgence of inflation threatened the already fragile external value of the dollar and barred the way to policies for a speedier recovery. Thus, to many people, the key policy decision was the imposition of direct curbs on the behavior of prices, wages, and rents. With these curbs in place, it was possible to extend the scope of the total decision (1) to correct the international position of the dollar and (2) to stimulate the rate of economic expansion at home.

Opposition to Action

A considerable body of opinion, in and out of the government, was opposed to some or all of the three-part policy package: (1) devaluing the dollar, (2) stimulating the economy through measures to expand demand and increase productivity, and (3) imposing price and wage controls. The opponents of such measures felt that the natural process of inflation's unwinding was making slow but satisfactory progress, that the residue of inflationary behavior would eventually abate in the continuing context of excess supply capacity, and that, while the pace of expansion was slow, the rate of unemployment had crested and showed signs of turning down. As for the outflow of dollars to other nations, that was in a sense *their* problem: the proper solution was for them to stop propping up the exchange value of the dollar. In short, their prescription was a laissez-faire "leave things alone" or steady as she goes policy.

Clashing Views on Mandatory Controls

The sharpest intellectual clash between the activists and the proponents of passivity occurred over the issue of mandatory price and wage controls. This clash reflected an equally sharp schism within the field of economics itself. It is still going on.

At one extreme, some economists have preached for years that a modern industrial society can achieve both high employment and price stability only through the use of direct controls over the behavior of prices and wages, especially in those sectors which are dominated by large corporations and large unions. At the other extreme, the mainstream of economics has preached—for two centuries—that peacetime controls simply do not work and in fact can be counterproductive.

The lessons of history appear to substantiate the anti-control school. In 301 A.D., the Roman emperor Diocletian imposed his infamous edict which set wages and prices for hundreds of detailed categories. In spite of the death penalty for those who dared infringe the edict, the program was abandoned, in shambles, a dozen years later. The history of price and wage controls since that date has not been much better. They work for a while but either break down in time (frequently with a large bubble of post-control inflation) or, if enforced by police-state methods, they lead to a severe misallocation of economic resources and a loss of personal freedoms.

The trouble with the debate on controls is that the discussion frequently gets pushed into its most extreme form. Those who are for controls tend to argue that they are permanently essential, clearly feasible, and fundamentally good. Those who are against controls tend to argue that they are never essential, always infeasible, and fundamentally evil.

That tendency toward extreme positions reflects the fact that serious debate in economics invariably allows itself to become dominated by an underlying clash in philosophies. And clearly there are more philosophies to be found at Harvard and the University of Chicago than are dreamt of in the universe of pure economic analysis. The pragmatic issue in 1971 was not whether controls were good or bad in any eternal sense, but whether they might at some particular time, such as mid-1971, do some good toward cooling the counterproductive price and wage behavior that was taking place. Almost everyone concerned was willing to acknowledge that wage and price behavior was *not* the initiating *cause* of inflation. Rather, the initial cause was an excessively expansionary fiscal policy which had first led to an excessive increase in the U.S. money supply and then, via fixed exchange rates, to an excessive increase in the world's money supply. The behavior of wages and prices in 1971 itself was originally only a symptom. But symptoms themselves can cause still more symptoms, as any good doctor knows.

The orthodox prescription was to remove the original cause of the problem (excess demand) and wait for the results. That prescription ignored at least one of two complications that frequently arise.

Symptoms such as wage-price pressures arising from the original cause might themselves lead to an acceleration of inflationary manifestations. The orthodox response to this problem runs as follows: Deprived of demand backed by money, such inflationary wage-price pressure cannot and will not last. Companies and labor groups which keep raising prices and wages will sooner or later confront a declining demand for their services. When that happens, they will behave.

But that response leads to the second complication: For how long should this confrontation be continued? One year? Two years? Even longer? One weakness of economics is that it has not incorporated a clear sense of calendar time into its otherwise powerful system of analysis. In economics, the "long run," by definition, is when maladjustments have worked themselves out. The process is clear enough but the calendar dimension is not. As Keynes put it, in the long run we are all dead.

When the first Nixon Administration took over the economic mess it inherited from its predecessors, the selected prescription was both "orthodox" and "compassionate": a gradual removal of inflation's causes until the economy returned to a non-inflationary but still expanding track. I remember, at that time, calling it a "Portuguese bull fight scenario." The Portuguese, unlike the Spaniards, do not kill the bull. But what if the bull refuses to leave the ring peacefully?

In mid-1971, two and a half years after the bull fight began, there was clear and disquieting evidence that the bull was still in the ring. To return to our other metaphor, the symptoms of inflationary behavior were still widespread and by some measures were increasing even though total industrial production was still below the level achieved at the crest of the preceding business cycle. It was in this context that wages, prices, and rents were frozen in August 1971.

Did Controls Work?

The 90-day period of the price-wage freeze was referred to as Phase I. It provided the kind of benevolent shock treatment the economy needed. Large group action is an established way of stopping the counterproductive behavior of small groups and individuals. We acknowledge this, for example, when we exhort small children caught in a fire to "walk, don't run." We acknowledge it when we insist that cars on superhighways run in lanes and within specified speed limits. In the context of 1971, the freeze, or Phase I, was simply an extension of those well-understood rules. It worked. By and large it was popular.

But why 90 days? This was the minimum time deemed necessary to prepare a less rigid, more durable system of administered controls. It was also felt that the goodwill essential to a total freeze could last no longer than a 90-day maximum. Whenever one chooses to start a freeze, someone is just about to get a wage or price increase, and that someone is likely to shout "foul." Unless a time limit is placed on his suffering, the freeze itself will not be widely supported. In a largely self-enforced system (somewhat similar to our income tax system), widespread support is a necessary condition for something as rigid as a freeze to work.

The idea of a 90-day freeze to be followed by a more flexible system called Phase II was not the only alternative put forward. Some were in favor of a six-month freeze, accompanied by a great deal of presidential preaching about the self-defeating nature of arbitrary wage and price escalations, and followed by a return to a system of market-determined prices and wages. Looking back, this prescription might have worked better over the long haul. But the concept of a 90-day freeze followed by a period of less rigid controls won out.

In any event, the policies adopted in August 1971 worked extremely well, at least until the end of 1972. Employment grew rapidly, with unemployment falling from 6 percent in mid-1971 to 5 percent by year-end 1972; man-days lost from strikes declined to a very low level; unit labor costs stabilized; real wages rose handsomely; profits expanded; the balance of trade and payments eventually improved. Above all, the rate of wage and price increases abated. In the final quarter of 1972, in spite of rapid economic expansion, the general price level rose at an annual rate of less than $3\frac{1}{2}$ percent.

As far as cost-price inflation was concerned, the U.S. economy was once again the best performing economy in the world between December 1971 and December 1972. Many official and unofficial visitors from the United Kingdom, Canada, and other nations visited Washington to see how we had "done it."

While many things went well for the economy in late 1971 and 1972, there were also a number of developments working against the success of our stabilization policy. Some of those developments, like the gradual erosion of public goodwill, arose from within the control system itself. Other developments, such as the overstimulation of economic expansion, were indirectly connected with the control system; they could have been avoided, but were not. Finally, still other developments, notably the massive crop failures of 1972, were just plain bad luck. The joint effects of these adverse developments in 1973 and early 1974 left the control system in a state of shambles by the time it was abandoned in April 1974 when the legislation empowering controls expired.

The Breakdown of Controls

When controls were first imposed in mid-1971, the underlying circumstances favored their success. Present were a significant margin of excess capacity in the economy, considerable public goodwill and support, and an abundant supply of most raw materials—including food. One by one all these favorable circumstances changed.

The erosion of goodwill. Not all wage and price increases are inflationary. To work efficiently, a system like ours must allow changes in some wages and prices in order to balance out the demand and supply for the millions of products and skills traded in the vast marketplace we call the economy. When inflation is not a national issue, nobody notices these continuous price responses to changes in tastes, technology, and seasons. When inflation *is* an issue, and especially when mandated controls are in force, everybody notices any change in relative prices and wages—if not directly, through the eyes of the all-seeing television networks. It is difficult enough for an expert to distinguish between changes that are legitimate and those which represent a breach of the control system; it is virtually impossible for the public at large to do so. With time, the list of price and wage changes that should and do occur gets longer, and so undoubtedly does the list of changes that do occur but shouldn't. Confidence that the system is working equitably erodes as both lists lengthen. The erosion of that confidence leads to an erosion of goodwill.

Any control system can suppress some of the larger price changes that might otherwise occur, even though they may be legitimate, in order to serve the larger interest of maintaining confidence in the total system. But these actions can lead to other, more costly distortions. Such distortions occurred in 1972, most notably in the lumber industry, but elsewhere as well. Exceptions, exemptions, and special regulations can handle a few of the individual problems, but the task becomes increasingly difficult as their numbers increase and as each correction breeds the need for several other corrections. In the process, what begins as a simple and well understood system, perceived by most people to be equitable, gradually loses these qualities.

There is another reason why controls lose some goodwill, even if they succeed—indeed especially *when* they succeed. This reason involves the function of organized unions. If everybody does in fact adhere to mandated wage guidelines, the adherence emasculates the very function of union leadership. What does the leadership do when everybody in or outside a particular union is going to get a $5\frac{1}{2}$ percent wage increase, and *knows* that he is going to get a $5\frac{1}{2}$ percent increase, no matter what union leadership does!

As the volume of inequities, distortions, and ill will generated by controls mounted, it became clear that Phase II of the control system could not survive without major revisions in its rules, regulations, and pro-

'Stick 'em up!'

Drawing by Bob Sullivan
Courtesy *Worcester* (Mass.) *Telegram*

cedures. These revisions could have tightened the control system by providing for a far more detailed and elaborate intervention into private decisions, administered and enforced by a vastly larger staff. A move in this direction was rejected for ideological as well as pragmatic reasons. Instead, a looser and more voluntary system called Phase III was installed in January 1973.

The acceleration of the boom. A second development which led to the eventual breakdown of controls was the rapid acceleration of economic expansion. During the last quarter of 1972 and the first quarter of 1973 that expansion turned into a super-boom, not just in the U.S. but in virtually every other major economy as well. There is no exact way of knowing how large a part the apparent protection provided by the existence of controls played in fostering the super-boom. There is a probability that it might have occurred anyway. But the larger probability is that the controlled behavior of U.S. wages and prices in 1972 induced a more expansive policy than might otherwise have prevailed.

Whatever its cause, the boom which started in early 1972 became an extremely powerful one. The early phase of recovery from a business recession is typically quite strong. This was not the case, however, in the early phases of the 1970-71 recovery. Between the summer of 1970 and the summer of 1971, industrial production barely grew at all. The switch to a more expansive policy in the summer of 1971 accelerated the rise in industrial production to a rapid 9 percent rate. For the half-year following the summer of 1972, the expansion accelerated further to the unsustainable rate of 12 percent a year. At that extraordinary rate, the U.S. economy was rapidly pushed back to the zone of its full capacity by the first quarter of 1973.

A similar acceleration in output and income occurred in all of the major economies. The following table shows the annualized rate of expansion in industrial activity between the summer quarter of 1972 and the first quarter of 1973; it also shows how abnormally high that rate was as compared to each country's normal growth rate. Industrial activity is a *physical* measure and thus does not reflect the effect of increasing prices.

Table 3. Growth of Industrial Production (Percent per annum)

	Average Annual Rate 1969-73	Rate from 3rd Quarter 1972-1st Quarter 1973
Belgium	4.5%	17.5
Canada	5.5	16.8
France	6.5	13.1
Germany	4.5	14.2
Italy	4.8	13.1*
Japan	9.5	25.0
Netherlands	8.5	13.1
United Kingdom	1.0	9.7
United States	2.5	12.0

* Italian rate is from 3rd quarter 1972 to 2nd quarter 1973.

The development of a super-boom had two effects relevant to the U.S. control system:

1. It pushed up the level of demand rapidly enough to create conditions of excess demand in many major sectors of the economy. Controls might serve a useful function when excess capacity exists; in this situation controls may help subdue inflationary behavior that remains from a previous boom. Few, if any, economists believe that controls can work as well under the pressure of excess demand unless the scope of controls is expanded to include a rationing system; no doubt these few would be happy to see just such an extension of governmental power.

2. The boom was accompanied by another period of extremely rapid growth in the nation's money supply. Instead of mopping up previously created excess money or liquidity, the expansion of 1971-73 led to the net creation of even more liquidity, not just in the U.S. but in the rest of the world as well.

The spread of money creation. The spread of international money creation during the super-boom of 1972-73 further reduced the viability of the U.S. control system. The Smithsonian agreement had not fully corrected the overvaluation of the U.S. dollar. If it had, or more accurately, if it had been allowed to do that, then dollars would have flowed back to the U.S. again in 1972. The level of world liquidity would have fallen, which was exactly what *should* have happened in the interest of world price stability. As it was, after a brief period of strength, the dollar weakened again in 1972 because the U.S. balance of payments remained weak. Indeed, that balance worsened during part of the year, and the outflow of dollars began again.

The outflow of dollars in 1972-73 had the same effect as in 1971—it induced a very rapid expansion in the world's supply of dollars, which led in turn to an expansion of domestic money supplies abroad. As noted in Chapter Three, the dollar outflows eventually led to a second and larger devaluation of the dollar during the first quarter of 1973, followed by a period of floating exchange rates during which the value of the dollar declined even further, reaching its low point in July 1973. From the point of view of the U.S. economy, these developments created a huge expansion in the world's ability to purchase U.S. commodities and investments.

The size of the increase in the world's purchasing power is seen by looking at what happened between mid-1972 and mid-1973 to Japan, Germany, and France—the three largest free world economies outside the United States. The Japanese money supply (in yen) increased over 30 percent in those 12 months. The dollar value of each yen rose by nearly 14 percent. Hence the dollar value of the stock of money in Japan rose by over 48 percent. (This figure is obtainable by multiplying the increased Japanese money supply, 1.30, by 1.14, the increase in the dollar value of the yen.) The dollar value of the stock of money in West Germany also rose by just over 48 percent in that year, but the composition of the rise was different. The supply of marks increased 10 percent and the dollar value of each mark rose 35 percent. The dollar value of francs rose nearly 40 percent, consisting of a 13 percent increase in the number of French francs and a 23 percent rise in the franc's dollar value.

Those 40-45 percent increases in the dollar value of the stock of money abroad in just 12 months were an ominous development. If even part of that potential buying power were to be used in bidding either for U.S. products (such as soybeans or corn) or for internationally traded staples (such as copper or oil or sugar), the effect on the U.S. price level could be a devastating one.

Events Augmenting Inflation: Supply Factors

Apparently Murphy's law was working in 1972-73: if something undesirable can happen, it will! In Europe, Japan, and several other economies the need did arise to exercise their hugely augmented buying powers; the effect on U.S. prices was a devastating one. Several events stimulated that need.

Worldwide crop failures. Widespread crop failures in 1972 caused food production to drop by about 4 percent; even in the U.S., which was least affected, food output declined. The demand for food grows at an average of about 4 percent a year. The serious shortfall in world output left the U.S. as the only major residual source of supply for food grains and feed grains. World demand backed by the now greatly enlarged stock of purchasing power drove agricultural prices upward faster than the gloomiest pessimist had been willing to predict in 1972. Raw agricultural products were exempt from U.S. controls. Between December 1972 and September 1973, the average price of U.S. farm products jumped 46 percent, the average price of grains jumped 68 percent, and the average price of vegetable oils jumped 97 percent. These are absolute increases, not annualized rates.

The worldwide industrial boom. The worldwide boom in industrial activity increased the demand for most basic industrial raw materials, including those relating to energy, faster than the supply could be expanded, which led to intense price pressures. Controls and the threat of punitive action held down industrial raw material prices in the U.S. Even so, the wholesale price of crude materials did rise at 30 percent a year during 1973 and the wholesale price of manufactured goods at 15 percent a year.

Elsewhere in the free world, where countries were not subject to controls, the rise in industrial raw material prices was far greater. This situation led to the development of shortages in the U.S. economy. While imports were not subject to controls, there was the usual uncertainty about how fast the control system would allow these increased import costs to be passed on; exports likewise were not subject to price controls, so it became more profitable to sell U.S.-produced materials in the higher priced markets abroad. Serious distortions developed during 1973, including distortions between the price level of uncontrolled raw materials and the price level of the controlled finished goods sector, distortions between domestic prices and world prices, and distortions between the suppressed level of profits and the less suppressed costs of expanding supply capacity.

In 1974 after controls were abandoned, industrial prices exploded.

The cut in oil production. To top this all off, in October 1973 the Arab oil-producing nations imposed an embargo on exports of petroleum and products to the United States, quadrupled the price of crude oil, and cut their oil production. This removed the last small existing chance for preventing a serious inflation in 1974.

Inflation After Controls: Evaluating the Influence of Supply

During the period of tight controls from August 1971 to January 1973 (Phase I and Phase II), consumer prices rose at 3.3 percent a year. After Phase II was abandoned inflation accelerated sharply. Between February 1973 and February 1974 consumer prices rose by exactly 10 percent, but a very large part of this increase was due to increases in food and fuel, where special supply factors (such as the worldwide crop failures and the quadrupling of oil prices) were a controlling influence.

In analyzing inflation, economists have generally been reluctant to invoke explanations based on supply factors in particular markets. The standard argument is that a drop in the supply of one or more commodities can lead to a sharp increase in the *relative* price of the items in short supply. But this argument cannot, in itself, explain why prices *in general* should rise. As particular prices rise, demand for those products affected should shrink and thereby eliminate the price pressure caused by the supply shortage in that sector. Furthermore, the diversion of funds to buy those more expensive products (such as food and fuel in 1973) should lead to a lower pressure of demand in all other markets, thereby weakening all other prices. This, in turn, should leave the *general* level of prices unchanged.

Recent experience has shown that supply factors *can* and *do* have a powerful inflationary impact. In affluent societies, the volume of demand is notoriously *insensitive* to changes in price, especially in the short run, and the price level for products and services is equally insensitive to changes in demand. Some shifts in demand do appear—for example, the demand for new houses and new cars fell sharply during 1973-74. But this decline in demand certainly did not generate any price declines for these two products. Instead, there were staggering increases. Therefore, it is not incorrect to assert that the supply-induced increases in food and fuel prices did produce a marked acceleration in inflation. Obviously the pull of demand backed by an enlarged supply of money was there as a necessary condition for what happened. But it was the fall in the supply of food and fuel which triggered the active use of that money supply in 1973 and 1974.

Inflation's Component Parts

In order to understand the nature of the 10 percent inflation we experienced between February 1973 and February 1974, and the change which has taken place in the nature of inflation since February 1974, it is useful to divide the total inflation rate into two parts:

1. The first is old-fashioned raw material or commodity inflation caused by a relative shortfall in the supply of food and fuel. This form of inflation tends to correct itself eventually if policies to increase supply are successful.

2. The second form of inflation is cost-push or wage-push inflation, which affects the prices of final goods and services. This type of inflation is caused by the pass-through into prices of rising raw material costs and of actual or anticipated wage increases in excess of productivity gains.

Over the 12-month period from February 1973 to February 1974, U.S. wholesale prices, which are much more sensitive to commodity inflation, rose by 20 percent and U.S. consumer prices by 10 percent. The relative effects of commodity-type inflation and cost-push inflation on the behavior of consumer prices can best be seen by separating the 10 percent rise into three parts: food, fuel, and all other commodities. That separation is shown in Table 4 for both the Consumer Price Index (CPI) and the Wholesale Price Index (WPI).

Table 4: The Composition of Inflation, February 1973-February 1974

	Percent Change (Annual Rate)	Contribution To Total (Percentage Points)
Consumer Price Index		
Food (.25)	20.2	5.1
Fuels (.04)	42.0	1.7
Sub-total, food & fuel		6.8
All other (.71)	4.5	3.2
Total Index (1.00)		10.0
Wholesale Price Index		
Farm products & feeds (.31)	26.8	8.3
Fuels (.10)	76.0	7.6
All other (.59)	7.5	4.4
Total Index (1.00)		20.3

The set of decimal figures next to the main component items shown in the first column is the relative *weight* of the item in the total official index. (For example, in the Consumer Price Index, "Food (.25)" means that food purchases, including meals eaten out, represent 25 percent of the typical consuming family's spending.) The second column shows the rate at which the average price of food *rose* during the period in question; e.g., retail food prices increased by 20.2 percent. The third column shows the effect which the increase in food prices, in itself, would have had on the total Consumer Price Index; e.g., if all other prices except food had been constant between February 1973 and February 1974, the 20.2 percent rise in food value alone would have raised the total index by 5.1 percent. This figure is obtained by multiplying the foodweight of .25 by the food price increase of 20.2, which gives 5.1. Doing the same thing with the fuel component (which accounts for 4 percent of the CPI) shows that the 42 percent rise in retail fuel prices alone would have caused a 1.7 percentage point increase in the total index.

Thus the inflation we experienced from February 1973 to February 1974 was dominated by just two items, food and fuel, which incurred huge price increases caused by a shortfall in their supply. Of the total 10 percent increase in consumer prices, over two-thirds (6.8 percent) was due just to food and fuel. All of the other items in the index (which account for 71 percent of the consumer's dollar) rose at the *relatively* modest rate of 4½ percent and accounted for less than one-third (3.2 percent) of the overall price rise.

Several reasons account for the relatively modest rate of inflation during this February 1973-74 period in non-food, non-fuel commodities and services:

1. Raw materials represent a much larger part of the total value of food and fuel products than they do in other products. Instead, prices of non-food, non-fuel items in the Consumer Price Index tend to be more influenced by factors such as wage rates, productivity, transport costs, and taxes.

2. Average wages rose at a relatively modest rate between February 1973 and February 1974: The increase in total man-hour compensation (which includes wages as well as fringe benefits) was about 6½ percent. Because controls remained in force for large sectors of the economy, the average price increase in those sectors was also suppressed.

These conditions changed dramatically after the first quarter of 1974. The spread of raw material inflation during a period of controls had created major dislocations in the total price structure: Wage increases had not kept pace with the huge 10 percent rise in living costs (caused mainly by "outside" factors affecting the costs of food and fuel). Workers who had suffered losses in real income therefore wanted, and were prepared to bargain for, much larger wage and compensation increases. Most companies had also suffered from a squeeze on profit margins. The cost of most raw materials had risen rapidly. So had the cost of labor per unit of output, which was up by over 9 percent, because man-hour compensation rose about 6½ percent and also because average productivity per man-hour had fallen nearly 2 percent in the context of a generally sluggish economy. Finally, companies knew that they faced a predictable acceleration in wage demands.

Thus, in the first quarter of 1974, the stage was set for an across-the-board increase in both wages and prices. Those explosive increases began immediately after wage and price controls expired. The rate of wage increases more than doubled from under 5 percent a year in the first quarter of 1974 to over 11 percent a year in the third quarter. The rate of increase in total compensation rose from 6½ percent a year to nearly 15 percent. Excluding food and fuel, average wholesale prices jumped by 40 percent a year. Thus after February 1974, the composition of inflation shifted away from the commodity-type which dominated thé period prior to February 1974 and toward the cost-push type. That shift is shown in Table 5, which covers the six-month period February 1974 to August 1974.

Table 5: The Composition of Inflation, February 1974-August 1974

	Percent Change (Annual Rate)	Contribution To Total (Percentage Points)
Consumer Price Index		
Food (.25)	4.9	1.2
Fuels (.04)	24.5	1.0
Sub-total, food & fuel		2.2
All other (.71)	13.9	9.9
Total index		12.1
Wholesale Price Index		
Farm Products & Feeds (.31)	5.0	1.6
Fuels (.10)	2.0	0.2
All other (.59)	40.7	24.0
Total Index (1.00)		25.8

During this period the overall rise in the Consumer Price Index increased to 12.1 percent a year. (All rates shown are on an annualized basis.) But by mid-1974 food was no longer the major culprit: food prices rose at a rate of only 5 percent (wholesale) and 4.9 percent (retail), thereby contributing only 1.2 points to the rise in the Consumer Price Index. Fuel prices almost stabilized at the wholesale level, but the pass-through of previous increases pushed retail fuel prices up at 24.5 percent a year. However, the contribution of the fuel price increase to the total rise in the Consumer Price Index was just 1.0 point.

The rest of the index, which had been relatively well-behaved prior to February 1974, shows a rapid acceleration. Prices of all wholesale items other than food and fuel rose at an annual rate of over 40 percent. At the consumer level, non-food, non-fuel goods and services, which account for over 70 percent of the things consumers buy, rose at a 13.9 percent rate and contributed 9.9 points to the total 12.1 percent consumer inflation we experienced.

The basic cause of the inflation was the huge increase in the supply of money which accompanied the super-boom of 1971-73. The first big manifestation of inflation up to early 1974 was raw material inflation centered on food and fuel. The big manifestation of inflation in 1974 turned out to be widespread cost-push inflation in most of the industrial sectors. At the same time, the economy itself moved into a recession. The policy problem had moved full cycle back to the dilemma it had faced in 1969 and 1970—on the one hand we faced accelerating cost-push inflation arising from wage and price increases and on the other an economic recession and rising unemployment. This time the two horns of the dilemma were even sharper than they had been in 1970.

Somebody once suggested a simple measure for total economic discomfort—just add the inflation rate to the unemployment rate! By this measure our Discomfort Index in 1965 was 6; in 1970 it was 11; in October 1974 it was 18 and still rising!

Drawing by Frueh; copr. 1932, 1960
The New Yorker Magazine, Inc.

Just around the corner

CHAPTER FIVE

RECESSION OR WORSE?

THE ECONOMY SUFFERED both inflation and recession in 1974. Economic activity declined and unemployment rose even as price increases accelerated. Those who like synthetic words call this unhappy condition "stagflation"—a combination of stagnant economic conditions and inflation. *The Economist* of London, which prefers lumpier words, calls it "slumpflation." Whatever its name, it is an uncomfortable situation which presents policymakers with a cruel choice: policies that might improve one ailment generally worsen the other.

Analyzing the Recession

Analyzing an economic recession is a complicated task involving literally hundreds of variables. Documenting that analysis requires a mix of leaden prose and tables that most lay readers would find intolerable. The essence of a recession is that the total level of output falls because the level of demand actually exercised in the marketplace declines. The principal purpose of analysis is to find out where demand is falling, why the fall is occurring, and when it might end.

There are no official statistics on the chronology of recessions in the United States. The decision as to whether a recession occurs or when it begins and ends is made by a private research organization, the National Bureau of Economic Research, and its chronology is widely accepted. In making these decisions they look to the duration, depth, and diffusion of the downturn in economic activity. For example, a dip in the level of output lasting only one quarter of a year would not be counted as a recession, but a drop in output lasting two quarters would be so considered if it met two other criteria. To be counted as a recession the decline in activity has to be more than trivially deep; small fractional declines, such as the one which occurred in 1966-67, have not been recorded as bona fide recessions. Secondly, the downturn itself must be widely diffused through several major industries. For example, a prolonged strike in a single important industry could cause total economic activity to decline, but this situation would not constitute a recession for the economy as a whole.

The oil embargo in late 1973 and early 1974 presented an unusual problem for business cycle analysis. Because petroleum is basic to so many industries, the cut-off in supply forced a fairly sharp and widespread reduction in total economic activity. Nonetheless, if economic activity had sprung back to its pre-embargo level after petroleum imports began to flow again, the decline would not have constituted a recession. However, the evidence indicates that the U.S. economy was probably moving into a recession even before the embargo was imposed in October 1973—all the embargo did was to hasten and sharpen the decline. After the embargo was lifted, the industries most directly affected by the shortage of energy did recover somewhat, but the economy as a whole continued to move downward.

We cannot know what would have happened to the economy without the embargo. Clearly the embargo itself, and the huge increase in the price of petroleum which the oil-exporting countries engineered at the same time, had a profound effect on the course of events, as well as complex secondary effects: on inflation, on real income, on consumer budgets, on monetary policy, on interest rates, on the availability of mortgage credit, on housing, and on the demand for cars.

In any event, the preceding expansion in the level of economic output and activity reached a peak around November 1973, the month in which the oil embargo took effect. After November, the U.S. economy began a decline long enough, deep enough, and diffused enough to be called a recession.

Phases of the cycle. It is useful to distinguish the various phases the economy has experienced prior to and during this recession. The *rate* of expansion of the preceding business boom crested as far back as March 1973. Prior to that time the economy had experienced a very powerful upswing. Output had grown at a rate of 8 percent for a full year, twice as fast as its 4 percent normal rate of long-term growth. The major source of stimulus for that extraordinary expansion was a record level of expenditures on new housing and automobiles.

After the first quarter of 1973, that record demand for housing and cars began to subside. However, total output kept growing although at a low rate of 2 percent a year and the level of employment also kept rising. The expansion continued because the loss of demand in the weakening sectors, housing and cars, was more than offset by increases in two other components of demand. The net foreign demand for U.S. output grew rapidly and the rate of business inventory accumulation accelerated. By the final quarter of 1973, business was accumulating inventory at a rate close to $29 billion a year—a rate that was unsustainable given the fact that the volume of final sales to consumers had already begun to decline.

Total activity reached a peak in November 1973. The Arab oil embargo induced a sharp fall in economic output after that month. The level of output did not spring back after the embargo was lifted and oil became available again. Instead, it continued to decline. The high price of gasoline reduced the demand for automobiles both in the U.S. and elsewhere. The number of housing starts also continued to drop. As the inflation worsened, real consumer income began to decline and consumer demand in general began to fall off. The rate of inventory accumulation, which had provided an additional stimulus of $29 billion a year to production in the final quarter of 1973, fell to $6 billion a year in the third quarter of 1974. Net foreign demand for U.S. output also fell. As a result of all of these adverse developments, the level of total economic activity fell throughout 1974. The Gross National Product (GNP), with inflation eliminated, was nearly 5 percent lower in the final quarter of 1974 than it had been in the same quarter a year earlier.

The decline in output was accompanied by both rising inflation and rising unemployment. The rate of inflation, measured over a 12-month span, climbed from below 8 percent in October 1973 to over 12 percent in October 1974. The rate of unemployment rose from 4.6 percent to 6 percent. By October 1974 it was clear to everybody, including the White House, that the U.S. was in the midst of a deepening and widespread recession.

In October 1974, the recession itself moved into yet another phase, and expectations about the future were revised downward fairly drastically.

1. Between October 1973 and October 1974, the level of employment rose even though the volume of sales to consumers was declining. The reason for the increased level of employment was that business was voluntarily building up both its stock of inventories and its stock of

plant and equipment. At the same time, the rate of unemployment also rose because the labor force itself was growing faster than employment was expanding. However, the rise in the unemployment rate from 4.6 percent to 6.0 percent was a mild one, averaging about $\frac{1}{10}$ of one percent a month. In October 1974 the level of employment itself started to fall, as production was cut back and more and more workers were laid off because business was no longer trying to add to its stock of inventories. The rise in unemployment accelerated sharply.

2. Inflationary expectations were also reversed by October 1974. In April 1974, almost everybody assumed (quite correctly) that the prices of virtually all industrial materials were going to rise rapidly. By October there were widespread expectations that most prices were going to weaken.

3. As more and more businesses cut back on employment and new orders, it became clear by October 1974 that the recession, already a year old, was going to get a lot older and a lot deeper before matters improved again. Talk of a serious depression became more widespread.

Depression Anyone?

Until 1974, the word *depression* had almost disappeared from polite postwar usage. It has been revived recently, and not just by the perennial cranks who squat at the very fringes of contemporaneous opinion. During the final quarter of 1974, serious observers in many countries wondered aloud about the possibility that we might be heading into a real depression in 1975. Unlike the word recession, depression is not a technical business cycle term. It refers to periods emcompassing several cycles of recession and recovery—such as the decade of the 1930s—during which the level of economic activity remains at a low level even during the upswing phase of each business cycle. Within the decade of the 1930s, for example, the sub-period 1933-37 was technically an *upswing* phase of the business cycle (unemployment *fell* from 25 percent to 14 percent). Another recession occurred in 1937-38 (unemployment rose from 14 percent to 19 percent), followed by yet another recovery phase 1938-40 (unemployment fell to 14 percent in 1940).

The case for pessimism. The case for pessimism about the economy arises from more than one source.

1. For some people the price spiral generated by the interaction between commodity inflation in the raw material sectors and wage-price inflation in the industrial sectors reached a critical momentum in 1974; it could not be wound down gracefully. In this situation, if fiscal and monetary policies are kept restrictive enough to break the momentum

of inflation, these policies will bring about a deeper and even more protracted recession. If expansive policies are invoked to reverse the recession, the pace of inflation could rise yet another notch up the spiral. A further jump in the rate of inflation would surely lead to an even more dangerous confrontation shortly down the road. The free economies will then find that they have only two choices left—to accept an even more onerous dose of deflation and depression or, alternatively, to accept a system of total government controls over prices, wages, and profits. To use an analogy, the pessimists believe we are now in a bus that is traveling at high speed toward a precipice: If we keep going we will plunge over the brink; if we hit the brakes hard enough to avoid the precipice, half the passengers will go through the roof!

2. According to other observers, the biggest cause for alarm is the vulnerability of the international monetary system and the impending threat that it will collapse from the strains being placed on it by the huge flows of payments for oil. These fears are not unfounded.

In 1969, the total of all balance of payment deficits arising from current transactions of all the countries in the free world together was a small and manageable one. Virtually all of the non-industrialized economies of the world had minor deficits. The exceptions were Iraq (which had a surplus of $104 million), Saudi Arabia ($41 million), and New Zealand ($105 million). The total of *all* of those deficits was under $8.5 billion. The principal economies with *surplus* current account balances were the major industrial nations—Germany, Japan, Italy, the U.K., and the U.S. All of those surplus countries had highly organized private loan and investment programs as well as government programs through which they lent, invested, or gave money to the non-industrialized economies, thus providing the credit which those economies needed in order to finance their modest deficits.

In 1974, the world's annual expenditure for oil imports alone was around $110 billion. The surpluses accruing to the oil exporting nations, which are of course someone else's deficits, were around $60 billion a year. The nations accruing those funds do not have an organized system cf loans, credits, and investments for financing the deficits corresponding to their surpluses. They do not sell oil on credit but for cash. They do not invest heavily abroad on a long-term basis. Instead they tend to hold most of their net surplus proceeds in short-term liquid assets—a large part of that in the form of bank deposits. Several questions arise:

   a. Can the private banking system continue to handle the ongoing problem of accepting the large and expanding volume of short-term interest-bearing deposits and lend those funds out at their own risk to all of the deficit economies which need financing?

b. What happens to an economy, for example Italy, when it can no longer command the growing volume of private credit it needs to finance the oil imports on which its economy depends?

c. At the high 1974 level of short-term rates, interest payments will swell the annual current account surplus of the oil exporters by a huge amount each year. For example, at a 10 percent rate of interest, the approximately $60 billion of just 1974's surplus will itself produce an *added* surplus of $6 billion in interest alone—an amount that is almost as large as the total world deficit was in 1969! The accumulated surplus by the end of 1975 will be close to $150 *billion*. Rapidly, more and more economies will find themselves unable to borrow enough even to meet interest payments on past debt. What happens then?

d. Finally, in a world of floating exchange rates, some individual lending banks will find themselves facing the large risks of foreign exchange fluctuations on top of other credit risks. Some of those banks might then face a sudden withdrawal of cash deposits at a time when they cannot liquidate the loans they have made without incurring heavy losses to themselves or to those who owe them the funds. In this situation, bankruptcies could occur, and one bankruptcy could lead to another. Some of this had already happened by the end of 1974, with the oil money game in progress for less than a year.

3. For still other people, the fear of a protracted period of depression springs from a prior belief that economic activity inexorably moves up and down in a long wave-like cycle that repeats every 45 to 50 years, and that we have now entered the downswing phase of one. The phenomenon is known as the *Kondratieff* cycle, named after the Soviet economist who first wrote about it in the 1930s. According to Kondratieff, these long swings pervade the capitalist world and are clearly discernible even though their timing may be upset by external events such as wars. Thus, the long trend in economic activity was *up* from 1789-1814, *down* from 1814-49; *up* from 1849-73, *down* from 1873-96, *up* again 1896-1920, and *down* after 1920. That downswing was still in progress when Kondratieff was writing, but those who are prone

to believe in the regular amplitude of long waves estimate that this downswing would have lasted the usual 25 years had it not been cut short by World War II. The same chronologists believe that the latest upswing really began in 1945 and lasted till 1971 and that we now face at least two decades of sluggish economic activity.

The case against depression. The case for pessimism is plausible, but it is not very convincing. Although it is foolish to rule out *any* economic scenario as impossible, the probability that we will have a depression on the scale and duration of the 1930s, or even anything like it, is extremely small. There are simply too many basic differences between the world today and the world of the 1930s. Together, those differences provide massive protection against a repetition of the 1930s.

1. Policymakers now know where the economic accelerator is located in order to stimulate the economy. They clearly did not know this in 1930 or even in 1938. Indeed, our problem today is that we now know too well where the accelerator lies. The danger is not that we will fail to use it, but that we will be tempted to use it too soon and too strongly.

In 1931, with the real volume of economic activity *down* 17 percent from its 1929 level, with prices *down* 12 percent, with corporate profits negative, and the unemployment rate at 16 percent of the labor force and rising, the medicine prescribed by the then conventional wisdom was a sharp *increase* in tax rates! The tax bill introduced in 1931 and passed as the Revenue Act of 1932 imposed the sharpest tax increase in our peacetime history. We now see that tax increase as an act of sheer folly; nothing worse could have been done to bring a staggering economy to its knees. But at that time almost everybody thought it was the right thing to do. The idea, as the proponents expressed it, was to balance the federal budget and to prevent national bankruptcy.

Today, in the same context, we would *cut* taxes, and indeed we would do so long before anything like the 1931 scenario was allowed to develop. It took us the better part of a decade to learn the lesson that the brake is not the accelerator. We are not likely to unlearn this now.

2. Along with the major revolution in fiscal theory, we have also come to shed a number of collateral misconceptions which prevailed in the 1930s. We are no longer afraid that deficits associated with a *timely* use of expansionary fiscal policy will lead to national bankruptcy —a favorite phrase in the 1930s. (World War II disproved this myth, as did the deficits of 1958.)

We no longer believe, as we then did, that expenditures on government financed projects are either useless and wasteful or useful but intrusive into the domain of the private sector. We now realize that the government can undertake many potentially useful projects without displacing private enterprise. (The Manhattan project, the federal highway program, and the space program demonstrated this.)

We no longer believe that a loss of gold or other international monetary reserves should automatically trigger a policy of tight money and high interest rates, without regard for the policy needs of the domestic economy. Finally, we no longer judge the posture of our monetary policy by looking only at what happens to interest rates; we also look at how the total supply of money is behaving. (Milton Friedman taught us this.)

3. Unlike the situation in the 1930s, we now have a system of unemployment benefits and other income maintenance programs which cushion the financial burden of joblessness for most workers. These benefits also cushion the shock which declining activity might otherwise have on the economy as a whole. In the 1930s, any initial fall in output and employment became magnified as its effects passed through the system: output would fall, causing a decline in income, which would induce a further fall in consumer spending, which in turn would induce yet another fall in output. Given these linkages, we did have a vicious spiral which sucked the entire economy ever downward.

The modern system of unemployment insurance and income maintenance breaks the vicious spiral by insulating a key part of the process through which it is transmitted. Today when output falls, personal income does not fall to the same extent; in addition, tax payments decline, making after-tax income fall even less. Therefore spending does not fall sharply and the original decline in output, instead of getting worse, comes to a halt within a year or less. Since 1947, no fall in total real output has lasted more than four quarters. It is likely that the downswing which began in late 1973 will be more prolonged than previous postwar recessions, but we know why; in this recession, because of inflation, tax payments increased even as output declined.

4. Our domestic financial arrangements are much stronger now than they were in the 1930s. We now have federal insurance on bank deposits to prevent the threat of losses to depositors as well as the counterproductive behavior and bank failures that such a threat then produced. Today, virtually all mortgages owed on homes, farms, and commercial buildings are subject to repayment in fairly small annual installments. In the 1930s, mortgages came due all at once just when it was impossible to raise the money to pay them off.

The Federal Reserve System now understands that its ultimate function is not to behave like a private institution but rather to serve as a lender of last resort, should that need arise. The Federal Reserve System faced the possibility of a liquidity crisis in 1970 (after the Penn Central Railroad went into bankruptcy), and it faced a similar crisis in 1974 when the Franklin National Bank failed. On both occasions, the Federal Reserve departed temporarily from its basic posture of credit restraint to provide enough additional lending power to avert a spreading crisis. These incidents provide ample proof of the Federal Reserve's willingness to act as a lender of last resort.

5. Our international financial arrangements are more enlightened than those of 40 years ago. In the 1930s, the deep and prolonged fall in output led to two forms of national behavior which made the situation worse for everybody. Each nation tried to protect its own producers from foreign competition and, at the same time, tried to increase foreign markets for its own products. The devices used were tariff barriers, exchange control, and competitive devaluations. Obviously *every* economy cannot succeed in the mutually self-defeating game of increasing exports and reducing imports at the same time. The major trading nations now recognize quite clearly that those "beggar thy neighbor" policies of the 1930s ended up beggaring everybody. They have agreed to resist any future temptation to indulge in such foolish behavior again. The cynic is likely to point out that international agreements tend to get broken when domestic pressures become strong enough; the optimist's reply is that nations do learn, even if the process takes more time than it should. It is true that individual nations, including the United States, have made some protectionist noises in recent years. Two unsuccessful examples are the Burke-Hartke bill and the recent bill (vetoed) requiring that 20 percent of U.S. petroleum imports must be carried in U.S.-built ships, manned by U.S. crews. But apart from the rhetoric, the larger trend has been toward more international cooperation. For example, even as all of the major nations were sliding into recession in 1974, the U.S. and its trading partners were preparing to move ahead on a new round of trade liberalization. Had it not been for the issue of Soviet emigration policies, this new round of talks would have begun in 1974.

While it is not impossible that the European Economic Community will break apart or that the U.S. would go back on the "understandings" that link our economy to others, neither development is at all likely. If either event does occur, it will not be motivated by short-run trade promotion tactics.

Taken together, the arguments for the case *against* a 1930s-style depression are far stronger than the arguments in favor of that unhappy outcome. If it becomes necessary, in order to prevent a slide into a deeper recession, the industrial economies will give up the use of restrictive fiscal and monetary policies as an antidote for inflation long before they accept even the *chance* of facing the 1930s again. The real problem in 1975 is not the threat of economic depression, it is whether we can get inflation to subside without imposing direct controls on prices and wages. There is hope even on that front, but given the recent propensity of Congress to follow rather than lead, the probability of that favorable outcome is not much higher than 51 percent!

Current Economic Peculiarities

One reason for the high level of uncertainty which prevailed in 1974 was that the course of recent economic events was quite unusual. The recession which began toward the end of 1973 is the seventh we have had since the end of World War II. As befits our peculiar age, it is also a peculiar recession. While every recession has one or more unique characteristics, our most recent downturn has many—and several of these represent important departures from previous postwar experience.

The two fundamentally new features of the current recession are (1) the presence of a high and accelerating rate of inflation in 1974 and (2) the oil embargo and the huge increase in the price of this basic and essential commodity. These differences have also led to a host of other economic peculiarities which set the current recession in a class apart from the other postwar recessions we have experienced.

Inflation. Generally the rate of inflation abates when economic activity slows. This time the rate of inflation accelerated. From mid-1972 to mid-1973, while the preceding business boom was in full tilt, consumer prices rose $5\frac{3}{4}$ percent. From mid-1973 to the end of the year, while the rate of economic expansion slackened to below its long-term normal growth rate, prices rose at a rate of $9\frac{1}{2}$ percent. Since the final quarter of 1973 the economy has been contracting, but the rate of price increases accelerated to over 12 percent. This acceleration in the inflation rate, in itself, has been a major reason for the decline in consumer real income and the subsequent reduction in the volume of consumer demand.

Supply vs. demand. Most economic downturns begin because demand falls off and thus induces a cut in production. We entered the latest recession with a plunge in output which started because the oil embargo, and the resulting shortage of petroleum, directly reduced the economy's ability to produce many goods and services (such as airline travel and petrochemicals) and indirectly cut off the incentive to buy others (such as motor homes and automobiles).

Consumer demand vs. non-consumer demand. In most economic downturns the initial decline in total demand starts in the non-consumer sectors. For example, three of the postwar recessions, 1945-46,

A brokerage house receives an order to buy ten shares of Goldman Sachs

1953-54, and 1969-70, were associated with large cutbacks in defense spending by government. The other three recessions, 1948-49, 1957-58, and 1960-61, were triggered by a fall in business spending for plant, equipment, and inventory. In the current recession a large part of the initial fall in activity was due to a decline in consumer demand, especially for new houses and automobiles, but also for the entire range of consumer goods. For example, new housing starts, which ran at an annual rate of 2.4 million in February 1973, had fallen to a rate of 1.7 million in October 1973, before the recession actually began, and fell even further to just over 1.1 million in October 1974. Automobile sales (including imports) peaked at an annual rate of 13 million cars in March 1973 and had fallen to a 10 million annual rate in October 1973; sales dropped even further to 8 million units in October 1974. In contrast, the volumes of defense spending and business spending for new equipment were as high in October 1974 as they had been at the peak of the expansion one year earlier.

Monetary policy and interest rates. Typically, monetary policy begins to ease after a recession begins. As a consequence interest rates decline and continue to do so as long as economic activity is receding. In the latest recession, the accelerating rate of inflation brought about an unprecedented tightening of monetary policy and an equally unprecedented rise in interest rates between March and September 1974, well after the downturn in the economy was known to be underway. Interest rates did decline between October 1973 (when the last cycle of expansion approached its peak level) and March 1974. But after March, monetary policy was deliberately tightened in order to combat the sharp rise in inflation which began at that time. As a result, interest rates rose extremely rapidly. For example, the prime rate of interest (i.e., the rate at which banks lend short-term funds to their most credit-worthy customers), which had declined from 10 percent in October 1973 to $8\frac{3}{4}$ percent in March 1974, climbed rapidly to a record level of 12 percent in July 1974, where it remained until monetary policy was again reversed in September.

Fiscal policy. In the typical postwar recession fiscal policy automatically becomes more stimulative as the level of output falls and unemployment rises. The reasons for this are twofold: tax receipts are closely geared to the current level of economic activity and therefore fall when output falls; at the same time payments *by* the government rise, especially for unemployment compensation benefits and other income maintenance programs. Both factors help to sustain the flow of after-tax income to the private sector. This automatic easing of fiscal policy did not occur during the first year of the 1973 recession. Instead of helping to sustain private income, fiscal policy actually had an opposite effect; the reason for the difference was inflation. Our tax system unabashedly taxes purely *inflationary* gains—and at progressively higher rates. The figures tell the story.

According to the official estimates, the total flow of national income grew from a rate of $1,118.8 billion a year in the first quarter of 1974 to $1,156.4 billion a year in the third quarter of the year. All of that dollar increase, and more, was due to inflation. In *real* terms, the national income fell. According to the same statistics, taxes *accruing* to all levels of government (federal, state, and local) rose from a rate of $437.3 billion a year in the first quarter of 1974 to $471.2 billion a year in the third quarter. Of that latter amount, nearly $15 billion was a result of the fact that most corporations maintained bookkeeping practices which *overstated* their taxable profits by the staggering sum of over $50 billion a year. One can appreciate the size of that quirk in our accounting practices by recognizing that *total* reported pre-tax profits were only $50 billion as recently as 1961.

The drag of fiscal policy on private income worked as follows. During the first quarter of 1974, the ratio of taxes (at all levels) to national income was just under 40 percent. But between the first quarter of 1974 and the third quarter, taxes took $33.9 billion of the $37.6 billion *rise* in national income—a tax ratio of over 90 percent. Thus instead of *insulating* the private sector from the fall in real income from which it was suffering, fiscal policy actually compounded that decline.

International leads and lags. In the six previous recessions we have had since World War II, fluctuations in U.S. economic activity have either led or lagged fluctuations in the other major economies. In the latest recession the level of activity in most of the major free world economies moved down in unison with us after October 1973 under the common pressure of a sharp cutback in petroleum supplies and the huge increase in petroleum prices. When national business cycles are out of phase with each other, the high level of activity in some economies provides support to economic activity in those nations that are undergoing recession. In contrast, when all economies move down together, each reduces its demand for imports from the others, which leads to a further round of contraction in all of them.

Changes in data and forecasts. The current recession has produced unprecedented revisions, both in the basic economic data and in the forecasts which flow from those data. Much of our economic information comes in the form of *dollar* numbers. But analysis of economic activity necessarily runs in terms of *real* changes, i.e., volume changes that exclude the effect of price increases. During periods of very rapid inflation, such as we have experienced recently, it becomes increasingly difficult to extract accurate information about the small real changes that are actually occurring from the huge changes we observe in the dollar figures.

Inaccurate information misleads those who forecast economic events. For example, in early 1974 a majority of forecasters projected that economic activity would recover in the second half of 1974. That forecast was based on two misconceptions. One was that the weakness in the economy in the first quarter of the year was confined to the energy-related industries such as airlines, utilities, and automobiles—and therefore that the economy would snap back once the oil embargo was lifted. The second misconception was that business had wanted, but had been unable, to build up their inventories because of widespread shortages in many key sectors of the economy. The implication was that the unfilled need to add to business inventories would keep production high even though final sales to consumers might weaken temporarily. Misleading data was a prime factor in this misconception.

The data were subsequently revised to show that business had actually accumulated far more inventory than was originally thought to be the case. For example, the original estimate of the rate of inventory accumulation during the third quarter of 1973 was $4.7 billion. That was later revised to $11.8 billion. The figure for the fourth quarter of 1973 was revised from $18 billion to $29 billion. The figure for the first quarter of 1974 was revised from $5.5 billion to $17 billion.

With these revisions, it became clear that the problem in mid-1974 was not one of too little inventory, but of too much; the assumption that inventory accumulation would provide a source of continued strength to the economy was rapidly replaced by the expectation that inventory liquidation would become an additional source of future weakness. Accordingly, forecasts were revised downward as the year progressed and fresh data provided fresh insights.

The Narrow Passage Out

During the final months of 1974, consumer and business attitudes worsened rapidly. Consumer buying plans dropped sharply and the sale of domestic cars, always a good reflection of consumer sentiment, fell to extremely low levels. Plans for new business investment spending, which had remained high until October 1974, were scaled back. Economic policy was also changed: the major policy objective shifted from an almost exclusive concern with inflation to increasing concern, and in some quarters alarm, about combating recession. However, a change in policy affects the course of economic events only after a time lag.

Given the existence of that lag, the decline in economic activity will probably continue, at least until the middle of 1975. By then, the recession which began toward the end of 1973 will have lasted longer than any we have experienced since the huge slide of 1929-33. It is also highly likely that the rate of unemployment during the summer of 1975 will exceed the previous postwar high of 7.5 percent recorded during the spring quarter of 1958. (The monthly unemployment rate reached 7.9 percent in October 1949, but for just one month; the rates for September and November of that year were 6.5 percent.)

The important question is what happens after mid-1975:

1. Will the economy continue to suffer from both a high rate of inflation in consumer prices and a high rate of unemployment?
2. Will we make a strong move to correct the unemployment problem and thereby exacerbate inflation even further?
3. Will we persist on the anti-inflationary front even if that threatens to prolong the recession beyond mid-1975 and results in an even higher unemployment rate?
4. Will we, in our frustration, seek to reduce both inflation and unemployment through a combination of expansive policies and the reimposition of price and wage controls?
5. Finally, can it reasonably be expected that inflation and unemployment will both recede on their own?

All five outcomes are possible, but only the fifth is interesting, because it represents the one clear passage out from our economic anxieties. Such a passage does exist, but it is an extremely narrow one. Today, an economic optimist must be defined as anyone who believes there is a better than 50:50 chance that the economy will in fact move through that passage into a less anxious state.

The logic which indicates that such a passage does exist rests on a sequence of six expectable developments. It runs as follows:

1. The first and crucial development is that the rate of inflation abates by mid-1975 to a level *below* the experienced rate of increase in spendable incomes. The reason for expecting such a development is as follows. The restraint imposed by monetary and fiscal policies in 1974 has reduced the level of total demand while the total capacity to supply most goods and services has kept on growing; therefore, most wholesale prices are likely to weaken sufficiently over the next six months to bring consumer price inflation down from the 14 percent rate we experienced in the summer of 1974 to half that rate.

2. The rate of increase in average wages has risen to the 10-12 per-

cent level and is likely to remain in that range for a while in spite of rising unemployment. When the declining rate of inflation falls below the rate of wage increases, *real* incomes will begin to rise again after an extremely lengthy decline which began in mid-1973. A rise in real income has two favorable effects: It reduces the pressure for large increases in money wages, and it generally leads to an increase in the volume of consumer purchases.

3. The prolonged recession we have experienced reflects the prolonged decline in the volume of purchases by consumers (the largest source of demand for economic output), which in turn reflects a prolonged decline in consumer *real* income (money income adjusted for taxes and inflation). The anticipated rise in real income can be expected, soon after it occurs, to lead to a rise in the volume of consumer purchases. When that rise occurs, total output can be expected to rise again and the decline in economic activity will come to an end.

4. Fiscal policy will automatically move in a more stimulative direction in 1975. In 1974, tax accruals rose rapidly in the face of declining economic activity. This unusual phenomenon was caused by a rise in the rate of inflation which increased taxable incomes even though real incomes were falling. As both inflation and production abate, taxable incomes, and hence tax accruals, will fall sharply. But government spending will keep on rising, indeed it will accelerate automatically, because of rising expenditures for unemployment compensation and other income-maintenance programs. As a result, fiscal policy will automatically become increasingly stimulative.

There is also the high, indeed almost certain, probability that the automatic swing to fiscal stimulus in 1975 will be augmented by a more deliberate set of expansionary actions. Tax rates will be reduced, especially for individuals. Expenditures will be increased, especially for large-scale public employment programs. The expectable stimulus from fiscal policy increases the probability that real incomes will rise, thereby increasing the chance for an economic upturn after mid-year 1975.

5. Monetary policy shifted from a policy of restraint to a policy of moderate ease in September 1974. The purpose behind the earlier switch to a policy of restraint in March was to reduce an over-rapid growth in the money supply. This purpose was achieved by September. In the process of achieving its goal, monetary restraint inevitably led to a sharp increase in interest rates, to a severe curtailment in the availability of credit, and to a large reduction in expenditures on such items as housing and public utility plants—both of which depend heavily on the availability of cheap and abundant long-term credit.

As monetary policy eases, credit becomes increasingly available and interest rates fall. Expenditures for new housing, which shriveled when credit was scarce, will start to expand again—thus helping to reverse the decline in total economic activity.

6. An important change in productivity occurs whenever the level of economic activity stops declining and starts to rise again. During a downswing in total activity, average productivity per worker generally declines; during the upturn it generally rises rapidly. The behavior of productivity has great significance for the behavior of costs and prices. For example, if wage rates rise by 10 percent and productivity *falls* by 4 percent, the labor cost for each unit of production rises by 14 percent. This is what happened in 1974. In contrast, if wage rates rise by 10 percent but productivity *rises* by 4 percent, the labor cost for each unit of output rises by only 6 percent. If a turnaround in the level of total activity does occur beyond mid-1975 and wage increases do not accelerate, we can expect a significant decrease in cost pressures, and consequently an even further unwinding of price inflation, during the early phases of the upturn in business activity.

If the policies adopted during 1974 do in fact lead to a tangible decline in the rate of consumer price inflation by the second quarter of 1975, the economy will have found its narrow passage out. Beyond the summer of 1975, recession will give way to a new expansion phase in which employment will rise again and cost and price increases will continue to abate. However, the level of both unemployment and inflation, though falling, will remain high by previous postwar standards. The passage out of 1974's anxieties is not only narrow, it is also likely to be fairly *long*.

What if we do not find the passage in the first place or, having found it, do not have the wisdom or patience to stay the course? What if the rate of inflation is still running in two-digit numbers in mid-1975, with the unemployment rate uncomfortably high and rising? The political drumbeat for wage and price controls, already loud, will probably become irresistible, and controls will be imposed. In that event, the larger watershed we have been crossing will mark yet another dividing line. The postwar quarter-century of essentially free market arrangements in the U.S. economy will have given way to an era of more-or-less permanent government intervention in the marketplace.

Control valve

Drawing by Don Hesse; © 1974
Courtesy *St. Louis Globe Democrat*
Distributed by L.A. Times Syndicate

CHAPTER SIX

THE ENERGY PROBLEM

IN OCTOBER 1973, with the imposition of the Arab oil embargo, what we now call the energy problem descended with great suddenty on the U.S.—so suddenly that it was immediately called a crisis. But the problem had been brewing for many years before it became boldly apparent. We now face issues which the President of the United States has described as "complex as the devil."

The public was not the only group to be taken by surprise. For two decades governmental policies had been fashioned as if the only big problems about energy were how to *suppress* supply and *encourage* its use. After years of assuming that a cheap and abundant supply of energy could be taken for granted, we awoke in late 1973 to the alarming realization that energy was going to be scarce and a lot more expensive. Over the past 20 years a host of policies and practices based on exactly the opposite set of assumptions have gradually become embedded in our system. The problem of turning these policies around 180 degrees is even more devilishly complex than the energy problem itself!

What exactly *are* the major problems associated with energy and energy policy? How did the situation we now face arise in the first place? How will economic forces influence the future cost and supply of energy, and how will those future costs and supplies affect the course of economic activity itself?

Identifying the Problem

The parts of the energy problem that we see most clearly, such as the large price increases which have occurred, and the tiresome lines at gasoline stations in early 1974, are just the tips of a huge and complex iceberg of problems. The high price of energy is a problem, but not for the obvious reasons. Our dependence on foreign sources of supply is also a problem, but not just because it might cause us once again to wait in line for half a tankful of gasoline. The energy question is a major cause of today's anxious economy because the problems run far deeper than the obvious manifestations which we see.

The price problem. When most Americans think of energy, they think of gasoline. Thus, for many people, the most obvious reason for believing we face a national energy problem, or even a crisis, is the fact that retail gasoline prices jumped by about 40 percent between the oil embargo of October 1973 and the summer of 1974. Including that large jump, retail gasoline prices in July 1974 were about 70 percent above their 1967 level. But does this fact alone create a national problem, let alone a crisis? Probably not. Although gasoline prices have risen faster than prices in general over the past year, the prices of a number of other individual items we buy have risen as much or more than gasoline over the past few years. As Table 6 shows, these include such diverse items as domestic services, potatoes, toilet soap, and drive-in movie admissions. We certainly do not talk about a drive-in movie problem or a potato problem or a crisis in legal services. Why then do we single out energy? We do so for a large number of reasons.

Table 6: Consumer Price Indexes in July 1974

Selected Items	Price Index*
All items	148.3
Gasoline (regular)	169.9
Rice	246.5
Fish	216.0
Watermelon	176.5
Potatoes	238.6
Chocolate bars	191.2
Re-shingling house roof	200.3
Domestic services	185.6
Washing machine repairs	165.3
Toilet soap	178.2
Drive-in movie admission	167.3
Legal services (short form will)	177.8

* 1967 = 100

1. There are almost no substitutes for energy in the short run. We have to use gasoline in order to enjoy the benefit of the $170 billion or so we have invested in the 125 million gasoline-powered vehicles we own. While we resent having to pay the higher price for gasoline, we realize at the same time that the other even larger costs of vehicle ownership (most of which we have already incurred or would incur in the short run whether we ran our cars or not) would be completely wasted unless we do pay the higher gasoline price. This lack of a feasible alternative leaves us frustrated. It is one reason the gasoline price increase is a national problem whereas the even larger price increase for other commodities is not.

2. The huge price increases we have suffered affect not just one or two forms of energy but all of them. The proximate cause of the jump in petroleum prices was the large and arbitrary increase exacted by the cartel of 12 oil-exporting nations known as OPEC (Organization of Petroleum Exporting Countries). But the price of energy from most non-OPEC sources has risen just as dramatically. In fact, the increase in the wholesale price of coal, which we produce ourselves, has been far sharper than the price increase of petroleum.

3. Energy represents not only a crucial element in modern economic output, but a very large part of it. Close to 10 percent of the annual value of our gross production and use of goods and services consists of energy in one form or another. The burden of the energy price increase is therefore not only unavoidable but large and pervasive.

4. Energy prices have been generally lower in the United States than in other developed countries. Furthermore, between 1957 and 1972 consumer prices for energy declined relative to the average of all other prices. Thus we not only enjoyed a very low price for energy relative to our income level, but we enjoyed a steady fall in that relative price. The recent sudden and sharp rise in the price of energy, which rose faster than the severe inflation experienced in the prices of everything else, came as a shock to a nation which had begun to assume that inexpensive energy was one factor it could count on in a world of rising prices and wages.

The set of circumstances in which energy prices increased is a second major source of concern. Most raw material prices swing violently in both directions. A shortfall in supply relative to demand drives prices up rapidly, sometimes by 200 or 300 percent. When demand falls off and supply increases, prices fall back again, equally sharply. Because most raw material markets are highly competitive, producers are generally unable to dictate prices.

The huge increase in petroleum prices after 1973 came about differently. Before the oil embargo in October 1973, the price of Saudi Arabian oil delivered on board a tanker in the Persian Gulf was $2.37 a barrel. At the time the embargo was imposed, petroleum production was cut by government order, and the price was raised to $7.60 a barrel. During 1974 it was raised in several steps to over $10 a barrel. At the same time the Saudi Arabian government took over 100 percent ownership and control of Aramco (the Arabian American Oil Company), which controlled virtually all of that nation's production, and which until 1973 had been 90 percent owned by four large U.S. oil companies.

The operating cost of extracting Saudi Arabian oil (excluding any return on capital) averages only *12 cents* a barrel. The difference between that and the artificial price of $10 a barrel set at the end of 1974 represents pure profit to the Saudi Arabian government. Obviously that $10 price has little to do with cost or with supply and demand—it is simply the result of a governmental decision on how high a price the traffic will bear.

In the case of most raw materials there is always the expectation, indeed the certainty, that such a level of profit will induce a large increase in supply and lead to a big fall in price. For example, the rapid rise in the price of soybeans, sugar, and copper in recent years were all predictably subject to an equally rapid reversal. This was not the case for petroleum in 1974. Saudi Arabia is the world's largest producer of petroleum and the world's largest exporter by far. So long as the world has no access to alternative sources of energy, Saudi Arabia can control the world price of petroleum by ordering a cut in its own production whenever total world supply increases by enough to put downward pressure on prices. The fact that their revenue from oil is already far in excess of their ability to spend it, even if they tried their hardest to do so, puts them in an even more powerful position. Saudi Arabia can very easily live with a 50 percent cut in production and export revenues for a year or more without making the slightest dent in her already huge bank balance. The world, including the U.S., could not now survive such a curtailment, at least not without a very serious cut in its standard of living.

Other producers of petroleum or alternative forms of energy such as gas or coal are not in the same dominant position as Saudi Arabia. They can set the price at which they choose to sell their output at a level *below* the equivalent Saudi price, but that would hardly affect the price at which Saudi Arabia could sell its oil, because, in the short run, some of that oil would be needed to meet the present level of world demand. However, other producers cannot set a *higher* price for oil (allowing for differences in quality and transport costs) without running the risk that they will be totally priced out of the world market, i.e., they would find no buyers. For example, if Indonesia arbitrarily decided to set a price of $25 on each barrel of oil exported but the Saudi Arabian government thought that was wrong, the Saudis could easily increase production fast enough to capture and supply all of the market to which Indonesia had expected to sell. In short, by 1974 Saudi Arabia had become both the key producer and the price setter in the petroleum export market.

Given this development, most of the other potential energy suppliers have simply followed the base price set by Saudi Arabia (adding or subtracting an appropriate allowance for petroleum quality and transport costs). For example, Canada has placed a large tax on each barrel exported to the U.S., high enough to reap for itself all of the benefit of the high price set by the Saudis, but no higher. Mexico did the same. Neither country is officially a member of the OPEC cartel. Venezuela, which is a full-fledged member of OPEC, prices its oil in much the same manner. The price setter is Saudi Arabia. Along with its two adjacent Arab states, Kuwait and the United Arab Emirates, it enjoys a combination of huge oil reserves, huge cash reserves, and a very small population.

The thought that the present high price of petroleum is not an "economic" phenomenon, in the strict sense of the term, is a troublesome one because it suggests that there is little short-run hope that the price will fall. In fact the danger is that the opposite will occur. If the Saudis decide in 1975 to raise their price yet again by 20 percent to $12 a barrel, there is nothing we can do about it which will not cause us more *short-run* economic damage than we can inflict on them.

National and International Aspects

The price of petroleum, and the near-term ability of the Arab nations to raise the price whenever they choose, is one major aspect of the energy problem. The other major aspect is that the level to which they have already raised prices can lead to far graver complications than the 55¢ per gallon price for regular gas which caused us pain in 1974.

A $10 per barrel price for crude Arabian petroleum has three immense consequences:

1. One consequence is that the oil-importing countries will have to pay about $110 billion a year to the OPEC countries for the petroleum they import in order to run their factories and automobiles. That represents a huge transfer of wealth even for the wealthy nations. The U.S., which is far more self-sufficient in energy than Western Europe and Japan, will have to surrender about 2 percent of its total an-

nual output to get the petroleum it needs—an amount about equal to all dividends paid by U.S. corporations. For industrial economies that are more dependent on imported petroleum, the proportionate annual burden is an even greater one. For poorer economies the burden of payments for petroleum and petroleum-based fertilizer imports is likely to be intolerable unless somebody else agrees to foot the bill.

2. A second consequence is that approximately $60 billion out of the $110 billion *a year* which the OPEC countries will *not* spend on their annual imports will be used by those governments to acquire financial assets in the rest of the world. As they earn interest on those assets, or as they raise prices even more, their net annual acquisition of assets in other countries will rise to over $60 billion a year.

How much can $60 billion buy? At prices current in October 1974, it can buy about one half of all the vast foreign investments U.S. companies have accumulated over the past 50 years, or the stock of all listed French and German companies, or all the shares on the London Stock Exchange (and with the change left over from that it could still buy all the shares of Exxon). It could easily buy all of the gold held by the U.S. Treasury, even at a market price of $180 an ounce. The thought of what a surplus $60 billion dollars *a year* could purchase over the next five years is even more staggering.

3. A third consequence is that the world will soon confront an unprecedented combination of economic power (over oil supplies and prices) and financial power (over world assets) within a handful of Middle Eastern nations, each of which is controlled by a handful of absolute rulers. Only an analogy can describe the situation that might soon emerge unless something is done to prevent it: One small monopolist group controls the water supply of an otherwise arid town; the group raises the price of water 400 percent, then raises it even more whenever it feels like doing so. At these prices nobody can afford to pay cash for the water he buys. But in order to receive water on credit it is necessary for the townspeople to acquiesce in four things: (a) never grumble seriously about the price of water; (b) never take steps to undermine the monopoly itself; (c) never ignore the monopoly's wishes on any matter about which it has strong feelings; (d) always allow the monopoly to use the funds it has accumulated to purchase whatever it desires from the town. This is the essence of just one prong of the devilishly complex energy problem—the energy problem proper. The essence of the other prong is that the townsfolk behave as if they believe they cannot do anything about the situation. This is not an energy problem, but rather a problem of energy policy. Before we can examine these policy implications, we have to understand how we got ourselves into such a position in the first place.

How We Got Here

There is an old joke about economists which goes as follows: Teach a parrot to say "supply and demand" and you have yourself another economist. The joke is not quite accurate. Today almost everybody who examines the energy problem (including geologists, engineers, elk-lovers, and Congressmen) talks in terms of supply and demand, but almost none of them thinks like an economist. The essence of economic analysis is its assertion that *both supply and demand are responsive to price.* An economist always talks about supply *at a given price* and what supply might be at some other price; he, she, or it talks about demand in the same way. Non-economists talk about what future supply and demand might be at *today's* price. As a result they are always finding "gaps" between supply and demand. When the gap is positive (i.e., projected supply exceeds projected demand) the non-economist's preferred solution is to curtail output in some artificial way; when the gap is negative (i.e., demand exceeds supply) his preferred solution is either to bemoan the inevitable imbalance or to correct it through rationing and allocation. For an economist there can be no lasting "gap" between supply and demand, only temporary ones; the equilibrating mechanism in which he trusts is a combination of price changes and patience.

Any discussion of how we got to where we are now uncomfortably seated—on the sharp prongs of the national energy problem—must begin with an analysis of supply, demand, *and* price. Before we can do this, however, we must find some way of dealing with energy as a single "commodity," even though it comes in many forms and is used for many purposes. Our major sources of energy are:

1. Natural gas—which is measured in mcf (thousands of cubic feet).
2. Liquid petroleum—which is measured in barrels.
3. Coal—which is measured in tons.
4. Hydropower—which is measured in kilowatts.
5. Nuclear power—which is also measured in kilowatts.
6. Miscellaneous synthetic fuels derived from coal such as "synthetic natural gas" (now called SNG in order to avoid the absurd contradiction in its original name).

In order to engage in an overall analysis of energy supply and demand it is necessary to express all forms of energy in terms of a single common denominator. Unfortunately, there is no one denominator that makes complete sense. Mass is meaningless and so is volume; dollar value is complicated and probably wrong because so many forms of energy have been subject to artificial price control. We are thus left with basic heating power as a common denominator. For that purpose we use the British thermal unit, or BTU. (A BTU is the amount of heat required to raise the temperature of one pound of water by one degree Fahrenheit.) The Btu is a very small unit of measurement and so it is necessary to record energy supply and demand in huge multiples of BTUs. One way to get around the irritating problem of zeroes is to think in terms of Qs, i.e. *quadrillions* of BTUs of energy.

Heat-equivalent is obviously not a perfect measure for energy supply or demand. Not all energy is valued for its heating properties; indeed, some energy materials are used for purposes that have nothing whatever to do with heat—such as the production of plastics. We also face the fact that electricity is a major form of final energy use, and the problem that the heat value of electrical output is far lower than the heat value of the energy materials we use in order to generate electricity. Which do we count, the *input* of BTUs of energy or its *output*? If we count BTUs of energy input in order to get a more complete picture of utilization, how do we measure electric power generated by hydroelectric methods which require no inputs of BTUs of energy? The answer is that we compromise—we count hydroelectric power in terms of "equivalent BTU" units.

Granted its imperfections, the use of BTUs provides us with a convenient single overview of energy supply and demand and thus provides a clue to how the size and composition of the two forces have grown. This overview allows us to analyze how and why we got to where we are today.

Energy demand. The demand for energy is roughly associated with living standards. It comes as no surprise that the U.S. uses more energy than any other country in the world; indeed we use more than one-third of the global total. However, we are by no means the highest energy-using economy if that use is measured in terms of BTUs *per unit* of total economic output. The list of economies which use more energy per unit of real GNP than we do includes a number of small countries such as the Netherlands Antilles and Guyana, which concentrate in energy-intensive industries; most of the Communist countries, which appear to use energy inefficiently; and also countries like the United Kingdom and Canada.

Growth in energy use is also associated with growth in economic output, both in the U.S. and in other economies. As far as the U.S. is concerned total energy use or input expanded at a slower rate than the volume of real GNP between 1930 and 1965. Thus, prior to 1965 the U.S. was "economizing" on the use of energy in the truest sense of the term.

However, beginning around 1960 the growth in our energy use has accelerated markedly, and for two reasons. First, real GNP itself has grown faster since around 1960. Second, and more important, our total use of energy *per unit of output* began to rise after 1966. Technicians have tried, without much success, to explain the rise in our Energy/GNP ratio since 1966; obvious energy-using innovations like air conditioning, electric toothbrushes, automotive anti-pollution devices, and the like account for only a small part of the observed rise in energy use per unit of output. A probable explanation, which appeals to the economist, is that the falling *real* price of energy (i.e., the price of energy relative to other prices) eventually induced a rapid increase in its use. For example, if the price of mechanical services rises faster than the price of gasoline, it may well pay a car owner to defer the cost of an engine tune-up even though such a deferral might increase his consumption of gasoline. Whatever the reasons, the growth rate of U.S. energy consumption clearly accelerated after 1965.

As Table 7 shows, total U.S. energy consumption (in BTU equivalents) rose at an annual rate of 2.7 percent during the decade of the 1950s, at 3.8 percent from 1960 to 1967, at 4.3 percent from 1967 to 1972, and at 4.8 percent in 1973.

The supply of energy. The accelerating growth rate of our energy consumption is one reason the U.S. energy balance shifted from a position of reasonable self-sufficiency to one of increasing dependence on imports. But it is by no means the only reason. What brought us to a critical situation in 1973 was an even faster deceleration in the growth of our domestic natural gas supply. That deceleration shows up clearly in Table 7.

Table 7: U.S. Energy Balance 1950-1973 (Quadrillion BTUs)*

Year	Total Energy Consumed	Domestic Natural Gas Produced	Demand for All Other Energy
1950	34.2	6.8	27.3
1960	44.6	13.8	30.7
1967	58.3	20.1	38.2
1972	72.1	25.3	46.8
1973	75.6	25.7	49.9
(Percent per Annum Change)			
1950-60	2.7%	7.2%	1.1%
1960-67	3.8	5.5	3.1
1967-72	4.3	4.6	4.1
1972-73	4.8	1.6	6.6

Source: Department of Interior, Bureau of Mines
* For those who prefer to think of energy in terms of millions of barrels per day of oil, one quadrillion BTUs a year has the heat equivalent of about 0.47 million barrels of oil per day.

From 1950 to 1960, while total energy use rose at 2.7 percent a year, the supply of domestic natural gas (principally from previous discoveries) rose at 7.2 percent a year. Thus the demand for all other forms of energy rose at only 1.1 percent.

From 1960 to 1967 the growth in total energy use accelerated to 3.8 percent a year. But natural gas, which grew at 5.5 percent, was again able to provide a more than proportionate share of our increased energy requirements. The growth in demand for all other fuels was therefore held down to a modest rate of 3.1 percent. In 1967 the U.S. was still essentially self-sufficient in energy.

After 1967 relative growth patterns changed dramatically. The growth of energy use accelerated to 4.3 percent between 1967 and 1972, but natural gas was no longer able to provide the disproportionate share of the increase in demand it had been providing. The reason is simple. Up to 1967 we were still finding and developing more gas each year than we were withdrawing. After 1967 the development of new gas reserves fell to a level below the rate of annual withdrawal; i.e., we were living off capital. Without the extra relief on the supply side previously provided by expanding gas withdrawal, the burden of meeting the growth in demand began to shift to other sources, including petroleum imports. As growing demand impinged on these sources, their prices began to rise rapidly. By 1972 the stage was being set for an energy crisis of some kind.

Between 1972 and 1973 energy consumption grew at the very high rate of 4.8 percent. The supply of domestic gas from our now depleted reserves grew by only 1.6 percent. The demand for other fuels rose 6.6 percent. Most of this increase had to be satisfied by increasing energy imports, which rose 33 percent in this one year alone. In 1973 the U.S. demand for crude petroleum imports jumped 45 percent. Almost overnight we had become the world's largest importer of oil and oil products, surpassing Japan by a wide margin. In late 1973 the impending crisis occurred. The price of imported crude oil was raised 300 percent.

Natural gas policies. While the symptoms of the energy crisis appear to be centered on oil, the roots of the problem lie in natural gas; that problem in turn can be traced to the imposition in the 1960s of federally mandated price ceilings on the well-head price of gas used in interstate commerce.

Natural gas is our cleanest fuel and the largest source of domestically produced energy. In 1972, for example, natural gas (and the gas liquids associated with it) accounted for 40 percent of U.S. energy production. (This compares with 32 percent for oil and 23 percent for coal.) Natural gas is also one of the most abundant potential sources of energy in the U.S.

Given the rising ratio of energy input per unit of real GNP, and given the increasing emphasis we have been placing on environmental quality, the proper course for a national policy toward natural gas would have been one that (a) encouraged its maximum development and (b) discouraged the very rapid growth in gas consumption, especially for purposes which do not fully reflect the full value of gas as a non-polluting fuel. The policies we pursued all through the 1960s did *exactly* the opposite.

The Natural Gas Act of 1938 specifically excluded gas production and gathering operations from the jurisdiction of the Federal Power Commission (FPC). But in 1954 the Supreme Court, by a five to three decision, extended the FPC's jurisdiction to include sales in the field by producers whose gas is sold in interstate commerce. The FPC grappled for years with the problem of setting ceiling prices for over 4,500 individual producing units and finally decided in 1960 to set prices by major geographic areas rather than on a company-by-company basis. After a tortuous journey through the Commission and the lower courts, the Supreme Court affirmed the Commission's first pricing decision in 1968. It is now perfectly clear that the ceiling prices set by regulation during the 1960s were altogether too low. The effects of an artificially low price were exactly what economists would predict them to be. The effort to find and develop new gas reserves fell off sharply. The use of gas rose rapidly. At the same time, more and more of what little new gas was found was diverted to the uncontrolled intrastate market (which was not subject to federal jurisdiction), where it was used for boiler fuel—a socially wasteful practice, given the growing need for non-polluting energy in the densely populated cities in the Northeast.

Today, after ten years of misguided regulation, there is a serious and growing shortage of natural gas. The shortage really began in 1968 when gas withdrawals exceeded new additions to reserves. But the FPC continued with its policy of keeping prices artificially low. The shortage worsened, and in 1971 gas pipelines had to curtail their firm (non-interruptible) commitments to customers by 500 billion cubic feet. In 1974 annual curtailments rose to 2.5 trillion cubic feet, or virtually one-sixth of the total commitments contracted for by the pipelines involved. Each such curtailment increased the nation's demand for the only alternative available—low sulphur fuel from abroad.

Although the FPC has recently tried to stimulate new production by raising the ceiling price allowed on new finds of gas, the basic policies that originally led us into difficulty are still essentially in effect. For example, in late 1974 the staff of the FPC recommended that the national ceiling price for flowing gas (gas found and developed prior to 1973) should be set at 24.5 cents per thousand cubic feet. That price, they argued, was not only fair and reasonable but it contained a large and extraordinary allowance to encourage more active exploration. The adequacy of the 24.5-cent ceiling price can be judged by two simple comparisons: (1) the price of gas in the uncontrolled intrastate market is about 400 percent higher; and (2) on a BTU basis 24.5 cents for gas is equivalent to a price of $1.37 a barrel of petroleum! It is policies like this which have brought on the energy problem. It is a problem that cannot be solved without a major reversal of practices and priorities. The social benefit of using an artificially low price in order to provide a politically popular subsidy to the fortunate few who get to use the available gas is probably outweighed by the social costs suffered by all those growing communities and industries who want natural gas but cannot get it because artificially low prices set by the government have reduced new supplies; it is definitely outweighed by the huge rise in the total cost society as a whole must now pay for alternative forms of energy.

Other energy policies. It is sometimes argued that we now have an energy problem because we did not have a national energy policy. This assertion is only partly true. The truth is that the large number of energy-related policies that we did have were not directed to what should have been their principal objective, namely, an assurance of adequate long-run supply relative to demand. Instead we have used energy policy, and still do, for all sorts of other purposes, such as the redistribution of real income among different groups in society. As we have just seen in the case of natural gas, the pursuit of these other objectives led us into trouble as far as the important *energy* issue, one of supply-demand balance, is concerned. If society really wanted to *subsidize* the consumption of natural gas (which is what Federal Power Commission price policy actually achieved) it would have been better and much less costly to society to do so directly. We now would be enjoying a more abundant supply of a critical fuel and suffering a less precarious dependence on the far more expensive outside sources to which we have been forced to turn.

Natural gas is not the only example of misguided policy in the energy field. There are dozens of others. Most of these will have to be reversed before we can hope to emerge from our basic energy problem. For our purposes one or two examples will serve to illustrate the point.

We now have a two-price system for petroleum. Imported oil, *new* oil (defined as oil from new wells), and oil produced from small "stripper" wells (defined as those wells producing less than 12 barrels a day) sell at free market prices of around $12 a barrel. The price for the rest of our domestically produced petroleum is controlled at $5.25 a barrel. The purpose of price control is twofold: to help hold consumer prices down and to prevent the oil companies from reaping large profits. At first glance the policy appears to make sense, but this impression evaporates as soon as one takes a closer look at the problem.

1. The policy tends to suppress rather than maximize supply. For example, assume I have a well producing 20 barrels of crude oil a day, which yields me about $105 of revenue daily at the controlled price of $5.25 a barrel. By making a small investment in well equipment, which I would normally make, I can keep on extracting 20 barrels. Without the investment, output from the well will fall to 12 barrels a day. Obviously in our two-price system I would *not* make the investment, because my 12-barrel well entitles me to the uncontrolled $12 price and thus *raises* my revenue to $144 a day. Alternatively, asume a company has a choice between two ways of investing a sum of money. The first way would increase production from "old" wells by 100 barrels a day. The second would increase production of "new" (uncontrolled) oil by 70 barrels a day. Which would it choose to do? Under the two-price system it would prefer the 70 barrels of "new" oil.

2. The two-price system also *encourages* price hikes by oil-exporting countries. Their only *economic* reason for any restraint on further price increases is the fear that at some price, demand might be significantly and permanently reduced because consumers would simply refuse to continue buying—regardless of how painful this course of action might be in the short run. But each time the oil-exporting nations add a dollar to the price of a barrel of oil, our two-price oil policy dampens the price effect felt by the consumer because it averages their price with our controlled price of $5.25. This dampening *increases* both the oil exporters' ability and their willingness to keep raising their prices. Our national purpose would be better served if our energy policies were designed to have exactly the *opposite* effect of what they now have. Many such policies have been suggested. The simplest would be to remove price controls on oil and impose a variable tariff on imports—the higher the oil exporters set their price, the higher we make the tariff, with the entire magnified cost-effect passed on to the consumer. It will hurt in the short run, but it will get us out of bondage within a reasonable time.

But what about the poor consumer, and what about the extra profits domestic oil producers will reap? Both can be taken care of quite easily.

We can cut income taxes enough to maintain the average consumer's standard of living, and we could finance that general tax cut with revenues provided by the oil tariff and by a tax on the excess profits that would accrue to domestic oil producers. Most groups would be relatively no better or worse off than they now are under the two-price system, but several important purposes would have been served. Domestic oil supply would be higher, consumption would be discouraged significantly, and above all, the level of foreign inhibition against increasing their prices every few months would be raised several notches.

Obviously there are additional ways in which U.S. energy policy must be reshaped in order to redirect it to where it should have been unambiguously pointed in the first place—toward the achievement of a better *balance* between the growth of energy supply and the growth of energy demand. Such a redirection of policy will not break the oil cartel in a day or a year. But without a major shift in U.S. energy policy, the power of the cartel to keep on extracting huge and rising sums from the rest of the world will be more strain than the world can stand.

The Oil Cartel

OPEC does not like to be called a cartel. For the first 13 years following its establishment in 1960, it did not think or behave like one; as recently as early 1973, OPEC was a weak organization which only a few people took seriously. Until then, oil production in its member countries essentially was owned and controlled by the international oil companies and oil prices, which were set by market forces, had *declined* relative to all other prices.

Starting in 1973 the situation changed dramatically. By the end of 1974 OPEC had succeeded in doing the following:

1. The governments of the major producing countries of OPEC had taken over, or were in the process of taking over, total ownership and control of petroleum production.

2. Sharp, government-ordered curtailments in output had been used, fairly successfully, for international political purposes.

3. Oil prices had been rapidly and repeatedly increased. (In early 1973 the price of crude oil in the key Persian Gulf area was $2.12 a barrel, of which the government "take" via royalties and taxes was $1.52 a barrel; by late 1974 the government take had been raised by mandate to $10.28 a barrel and the price to $10.50. Both the government take and the corresponding price were even higher at other OPEC export points.)

4. The OPEC countries were collectively extracting around *$110 billion* a year from oil-importing countries and accumulating $60 billion a year out of those receipts.

"As Adam Smith so aptly put it . . ."

The actions taken by the oil cartel since October 1973 have either triggered or exacerbated all of the major economic anxieties the world suffered in 1974—economic dislocation due to a lack of fuel, rising inflation, mounting recession and unemployment, the growing fear of an international financial crisis, and a worldwide collapse in common stock prices. The architects of OPEC may not have planned it that way, but by the end of 1974 OPEC had emerged as the most successful, powerful, and potentially destructive commodity cartel in world history. The future of all the free economies depends crucially on how the potential threat represented by the OPEC cartel is met.

The policy issues which have by now become built into the oil problem are more complex than anything the free world has faced before in peacetime. It would take an entire book to explore the complicated interactions involved. But two key points are clear enough to be stated in a page or two.

The central issue today is the degree of the world's future dependence on more OPEC oil. Between 1969 and 1973 world oil consumption rose by 38 percent, from 41.5 million to 57.5 million barrels per day (b/d), and dependence on imported OPEC oil rose by 45 percent, from 21.5 million to 30.9 million b/d. That phenomenal increase triggered the price raising power of the OPEC countries. If world demand for OPEC oil keeps on increasing, OPEC countries will keep on raising oil prices, cutting production whenever it becomes necessary to do so in order to make the next round of price increases stick. The present burden of $10 per barrel of oil is already higher than most of the world's economies can bear. Further increases in oil prices will lead sooner or later to a major breakdown in the world system of production, trade, and finance.

The only feasible *economic* strategy now available to the major industrial economies is for them to take strong and concerted actions to freeze their aggregate demand for OPEC oil at the level of 31 million b/d which prevailed in 1973. Such a result will not be easily achieved; the total demand for OPEC oil had been *rising* at $7\frac{1}{2}$ percent a year prior to 1973 and bringing that growth down to zero will require very strong measures indeed. But it can be done, and if it is done there is an extremely good chance that the oil cartel will break and that oil prices will drop significantly before 1980. Table 8 shows why.

Table 8: OPEC Oil Production

Country	Population (Millions)	Reserves* (Years)	Production (million b/d) 1969	1973	1974
Group 1					
Iran	32.0	28	3.4	5.9	6.1
Indonesia	125.0	22	0.7	1.3	1.5
Nigeria	74.0	27	0.5	2.0	2.4
Iraq	11.0	44	1.5	2.0	2.0
Ecuador	7.0		—	0.2	0.3
			6.1	11.4	12.3
Group 2					
Saudi Arabia	8.0	51	3.2	7.7	8.5
Other Arabia†	0.3	50	1.8	2.0	2.7
			5.0	9.7	11.2
Group 3					
Kuwait	1.0	66	2.6	3.1	2.2
Libya	2.0	32	3.1	2.2	2.0
Venezuela	11.0	11	3.6	3.5	2.9
Algeria	15.0	20	1.0	1.0	1.1
			10.3	9.8	8.2
TOTAL			21.4	30.9	31.7

* Years of reserves remaining at 1973 production rate.
† Includes United Arab Emirates and other minor states.

The Table divides the OPEC producers into three groups:

1. The group of "expansionist" states such as Iran, Nigeria, and Indonesia. These are states with relatively large populations and/or relatively large and growing needs for maximum export revenues now. All of them have been expanding output as rapidly as they can and are likely to keep on doing so because they desperately need the funds to pay for economic and/or military development plans.

2. The second group consists of Saudi Arabia and the minor sheikdoms on the Arabian peninsula such as Abu Dhabi and Dubai, in which about one-third of the free world's known reserves of oil are located. The capacity of this group to produce oil has been expanding extremely rapidly. Given the existence of large reserves, it will continue to do so. These countries do not have a pressing need for current revenue—indeed they can barely cope with the huge inflow of funds they are already receiving. On the other hand, the idea that *a barrel of oil in the ground* is worth more to them than *a barrel produced* is a myth invented by somebody who has never seen a compound interest table. Each barrel produced today generates $10, and $10 invested at 10 percent will grow to $1,175 in 50 years. A policy of deliberately leaving that barrel "in the ground" for economic reasons makes sense only if its owner can confidently expect thereby to push the price of oil up to at least $1,175 *a barrel* before then! The Saudi Arabs are smart enough to realize that long before the price of oil gets anywhere near that level the market for oil would disappear completely because oil would be displaced by alternative sources of energy.

Saudi Arabia, more than any other oil producer, has a critical long-run interest in the survival and prosperity of the free industrial economies. She owns the largest pool of oil reserves and therefore requires the most enduring markets for petroleum; she owns the largest and most rapidly growing pool of financial assets, most of which has to be held in the industrial economies; she has a greater fear and abhorrence of atheistic socialism than is true of any other producing nation. Although Saudi Arabia has frequently taken the lead in bringing about the severe price increases already imposed, her long-run interests clearly require a policy which aims at a maximum *volume* of output rather than a maximum short-run price per barrel.

3. The third group of countries, including Venezuela, Libya, and Algeria, have an aggressive interest in maximizing prices even at the risk of losing sales volume. Because their known reserves are relatively small and their producing capacities are on the decline, their horizons are shorter; they stand to lose little even if their current pricing actions cause the long-run market for OPEC oil to shrink rapidly.

What all the foregoing suggests is that, if the industrial nations act in concert to hold down their total demand for OPEC oil, OPEC itself is not likely to survive as a unified cartel with a unified set of pricing and market sharing policies. It will break apart as each group of member countries pursues its own interests. Indeed, that process has already begun. In order to maintain the most recent level of imposed prices, Libya has had to cut its output from well over 2 million b/d to under 1 million barrels, and Venezuela has had to cut from 3.5 million to under 3 million. By 1980 output in the expansionist group of producing states, which has already doubled from 6.1 million to 12.3 million b/d, is likely to rise further to around 18 million. If Saudi Arabia and the other emirates in Group 2 also expand even modestly, they could easily fill the remaining 12 or 13 million b/d of demand (assuming total demand is in fact held below the 31 million b/d level). The market for oil from the states in Group 3 will shrink to zero! Sooner or later prices will break —and once they break they are likely to break sharply. Even if the Group 2 and Group 3 nations manage to bind themselves to share production cuts equitably, the constraint of producing so far below their capacity to produce will eventually put huge strains on the agreement. For example, it is hard to envisage Saudi Arabia, whose capacity to produce will be well above 12 million barrels by 1980, holding its production down to half that level just to accommodate its cartel partners.

U.S. policy. If Saudi Arabia is the key nation on the OPEC side, the U.S. is the key nation among the industrial nations. It is the largest user of energy, the largest and fastest growing market for OPEC oil, and the largest source of the technology and investment required for the development of non-OPEC sources of energy. The objective of holding the demand for OPEC oil down to 31 billion b/d between now and 1980 requires strong, clear-cut leadership by the United States, and it requires that leadership by no later than 1975. To provide that leadership, U.S. policy and "politics" will have to give up somewhat on other objectives whose pursuit helped to create the energy problem in the first place. A few examples will suffice to illustrate the point.

Price. We have pursued a misguided policy of artificially holding down the price of two major forms of energy—oil and natural gas—and we are still doing so. Such a policy is politically popular but economically absurd. The temporary advantage the consumer previously gained from lower prices imposed on natural gas has been more than offset by the huge price increases that have taken place in the uncontrolled forms of energy. The temporary advantage the U.S. consumer is now enjoying because some prices are still being artificially suppressed also has a huge cost that can no longer be ignored; with such policies the crucial objective of reducing our reliance on OPEC imports cannot be achieved. The future cost of failure on that front will far exceed the minor political comfort which current policies now provide. Price is *the* major and natural incentive for energy conservation. It is also the major and natural incentive for increasing supply. Therefore all energy prices should be deregulated completely. Any inequities caused by a return to free markets for oil and natural gas should be corrected via the tax system.

Conservation. The incentive for conservation provided by market price alone is not likely to depress demand sufficiently rapidly. It should therefore be reinforced by other positive actions to ensure an even greater degree of energy conservation. Thus far, all we have done is impose a 55-mile-per-hour speed limit. Much more can and should be done. For example, ICC (Interstate Commerce Commission) regulations now require many trucks collectively to deadhead or detour by millions of miles a year. The cost to society of removing these regulations is close to zero. The use of taxes or tariffs provides another way of reinforcing conservation; yet, because they are unpopular, the U.S. uses such measures to a far lesser extent than is the case in Europe and Japan.

Supply. In addition to price ceilings, mandatory allocation, and similar restraints, present U.S. policy inhibits the growth of energy supply in dozens of ways. Some are related to environmental considerations, and most observers agree that some of these can be relaxed in the short run without serious cost to society. Other restraints are related to outmoded policy decisions made in the past. For example, the U.S. Navy holds billions of barrels of oil reserves within the U.S. in the form of "Naval Petroleum Districts." It hardly makes sense to leave all that oil untapped in the context of today's energy problems.

Unless the U.S. itself shows that it is serious about meeting the challenge imposed by the oil cartel by giving up on the pursuit of a long list of fairly trivial objectives, that challenge will grow. In a few years it will represent a far greater threat to the world's economy and welfare than all of the minor ills to whose cure we have mindlessly bent our energy policies over the past 15 years.

"I see a substantial upswing in the economy by October, but
who knows? Maybe it's the Valium talking."

CHAPTER SEVEN

A NOTE ON INFLATION AND STOCK PRICES

ONE THEME OF THIS BOOK is that the steady success of postwar economic policy, at least until 1968, led us as a nation to adopt a number of invalid beliefs and assumptions about the economy. The major watershed we have been passing through since 1968, and especially during the past two years, has been a sobering time of reappraisal on virtually all of those assumptions. One of the false assumptions we developed, which reached its apogee around 1968, was that common stocks provided a reliable hedge against inflation, and indeed that inflation was somehow a good thing for common stock prices.

The origin of the belief is simple enough. From 1949 to the end of 1968, a period of fairly steady inflation, the Standard and Poor's index of 500 common stock prices (S&P 500) increased 7-fold, from 15.2 to 106.5. The "real" value of the bundle of 500 stocks contained in the index, adjusted for the rise in the cost of living, enjoyed a $4\frac{1}{2}$-fold increase. The false conclusion which was drawn was that common stock prices would keep on rising, providing for investors a continuous hedge against whatever inflation might occur.

A collateral piece of equally false logic used to support the ever-rising stock market thesis was the argument that a "shortage" of good stocks existed relative to the rising demand for stocks. That shortage in turn was traced to the fact that there was a growing demand for stocks from the rapidly increasing accumulations of pension funds and other institutionally managed investments which could be satisfied only by bidding stocks away from individual investors. Again, the statement itself was correct. Between 1949 and 1968 common stocks held by pension funds and other institutional groups rose from a mere $13 billion to nearly $220 billion. Part of the rise was a result of the increase in stock prices, but much of it was a result of steady purchases by the institutions. Starting in 1958, and for every year since then, individuals have been net sellers of common stock. However, the conclusion which was derived from the facts—that the net buying pressure from institutions would keep on pushing stock prices upward—was obviously not justified.

Both myths—that inflation was somehow "good" for stock prices and that the continuous pressure of institutional buying would keep stock prices rising—were bruised after the present wave of inflation began at the end of 1965, and both myths have been shattered by the course of events since the end of 1968! The S&P 500 stock price index, which averaged 106.5 during December 1968, averaged 69.4 during October 1974. Adjusting for the huge inflation which occurred between 1968 and 1974, the "real" price of stocks had fallen by nearly 50 percent. Over the past six years inflation has been clearly "bad" for stock prices; stocks have provided a poorer "hedge" against inflation than almost any other major form of investment, and the fact that institutional investors continued to be steady purchasers of stocks from individuals made no difference at all.

Inflation and Stock Prices, in Theory

Why was inflation so "good" for stock prices between 1949 and 1965 (or 1968) and so "bad" after 1968? Nobody has answered this question in any definitive way. Theory suggests that any inflation rate *which is correctly and universally anticipated* by the financial markets should have no effect at all on stock prices!

The value of a financial instrument that represents a claim to *future* income (which is all that a common stock really is) is equal to the expected future *stream* of income, discounted at some rate. The rate of discount used in evaluating a particular instrument is equal to the sum of two things: the interest rate available on guaranteed claims (such as government bonds) and a premium rate which reflects the uncertainty of the future stream promised by that particular instrument. For example, if you offer me a guaranteed claim to $1 a year *forever* (to keep the arithmetic simple), if I can get 5 percent a year on a long-term government bond, if I believe your promise is as "good" as the government's, then I should be prepared to pay you $20 to buy the claim you offer to sell me, no more and no less. The $20 "value" of the claim is logically equal to the expected income stream of $1 a year, discounted at a rate of 5 percent per annum.

If I perceive your claim to be *less* reliable or certain than that offered by the government, I would have to *discount* your promise at some rate higher than 5 percent a year—how much higher will depend on my estimate of the extra rate of return I should aim at in order to compensate myself for bearing the uncertainty I perceive in your ability to deliver on your promise. For example, I may want 5 percent a year *more* to induce me to put my money in a claim against you than I would want from a more secure claim against the government. So, I would use a discount rate of 5 + 5, or 10 percent, in evaluating the $1-a-year stream of income you promise. That would give a price of only $10 for your claim.

Now we can add the inflation complication, but on the simple basis that *everybody* expects a common rate of inflation, e.g., 4 percent a year, to go on forever. Obviously everybody will now want 9 percent from the government instead of the 5 percent return they would have wanted in the absence of inflation. I would still want an *extra* 5 percent from you to compensate me for the relative uncertainty attaching to your promise as compared to the government's. Hence I would want 14 percent a year from you. But if my claim against you is in the nature of a *common stock* instrument, your "promise" is no longer a *steady* $1 a year, but one which will itself rise with inflation at 4 percent a year, i.e., the promise is a growing stream rather than a level one because the expected inflation will increase corporate sales and earnings.

Mathematics tells us that the value of a stream which continuously grows from $1 a year today, to $1.04 a year next year, and so on, discounted at (10 + 4) or 14 percent is the *same* as the value of a steady stream of $1 a year discounted at 10 percent. In short, if *everybody in the financial markets has a common expectation regarding future inflation*, then the inflation rate itself should have a *zero* effect on the price of common stocks. Inflation would be neither good nor bad for stock prices!

Inflation and Stock Prices, in Practice

The trouble with the simple theory summarized above is also simple —in the real world everybody does not project a single expectation about future inflation. Indeed the same person might project one rate of inflation when he thinks about one thing and an altogether different rate when he thinks about another. That propensity for doublethink leads to a great deal of confusion. For example, in 1950 a lot of people and banks were obviously happy to buy long-term government bonds that paid 2.31 percent interest a year. In 1956 they were happy to buy bonds paying 3.08 percent. They could *not* have been expecting any inflation at all in 1950, or 1956, or indeed over the succeeding 25 years. Yet in 1951 the inflation rate was 8 percent, in 1957 it was 3½ percent, and between 1950 and 1974 it averaged 2½ percent a year. As far as other projections were concerned, such as corporate prices, sales, profits and wages, the same people were probably projecting inflation rates closer to those that actually occurred.

In 1974 we witnessed an opposite phenomenon. In their capacity as bond buyers and lenders, people in 1974 behaved *as if* they expected very high rates of inflation to continue for decades. For example, they priced corporate bonds so as to get a yield of nearly 10 percent per annum over the next 20 years, much of that to allow for the *inflation* they expected. But the same people apparently did not believe that inflation was really going to continue when they evaluated common stocks. In fact, one reason common stock prices fell so sharply in 1973 and 1974 was that people expected inflation would end.

In short, inflation is bad for stock prices whenever the inflation rate gets so high that people know it must somehow be brought to an end. The worse the inflation rate gets, the less sustainable people believe it is, and the greater the trauma with which they expect it will end. History is on their side. Few major inflations in history have ended without some sort of serious loss of the value of property rights held by common stock holders. Many inflations have ended with permanent losses. As a result, every serious inflation has been accompanied by a large evaporation of common stock prices. Indeed, the large losses suffered by U.S. common stock holders since 1965 is the third such inflation-associated loss the U.S. has experienced in the past 60 years. All of it has happened before.

Inflation and Stock Prices—a Brief History

During the World War I period, the main economic variables, such as the GNP, corporate output, and corporate earnings rose sharply in terms of nominal dollars, due partly to real expansion but largely to a very high rate of inflation. By 1920, dollar GNP was over 2½ *times* as high as it had been in 1910, but the S&P stock index was lower in 1921 than it had been in 1909—in fact it was nearly 30 percent lower. In "real" terms, allowing for inflation, common stock prices were 63 percent lower! Stock prices then recovered to their 1909 level only in early 1925, and it was 1927 before the total value of stocks was once again consonant with the now enlarged size of the economy.

The same phenomenon occurred during and after World War II. By 1949 the U.S. economy, as measured by dollar GNP, was again over 2½ *times* the level that had prevailed in 1939, and again a large part of that expansion had been due to rapid inflation. Yet the S&P stock index in 1949 was *lower* than it had been 12 years earlier in 1937. In "real" terms, allowing for inflation, stocks were over 40 percent lower. Once again, it took the better part of a decade for the value of stocks to rise to a level commensurate with the economy.

What we witnessed in the 1950s and early 1960s was a "catch-up" phase in which stock prices rose again to match the size and profitability of the economy on which their value ultimately depends. That rise had nothing to do with institutional purchasing pressure or because inflation, as such, is "good" for stocks.

We are now experiencing a third major inflationary episode in which common stock values have fallen both absolutely and relative to the economy itself. By late 1974 the dollar volume of GNP was over *twice* the level which prevailed in 1965, much of the rise due to rapid inflation. Yet in October 1974, the S&P index was nearly 25 percent below the level which had prevailed nine years earlier in October 1965. In "real" terms, allowing for the intervening inflation, stock prices had declined 45 percent, a somewhat larger decline than we experienced during World War II, but less than the real decline experienced during World War I. Looked at another way, in 1965 before the present wave of inflation began, the total market value of common stock was equal to just about one year's GNP. In October 1974, total market value had fallen to just about 45 percent of one year's GNP.

Nobody can predict, with certainty, that history will repeat itself, but there is no good reason for believing it will not. If it does, the other side of the economic watershed through which we have been passing will bring less anxious times, inflation will gradually abate to acceptable levels, and common stock prices will climb again until their total market value is once again commensurate with the size of the economy.

© Collection of William G. McLoughlin, Providence, Rhode Island

READER'S GUIDE

NON-ECONOMISTS WHO ARE interested in following the course of economic events generally ask two kinds of questions about reading matter: (1) Where can I find a straightforward description of the concepts which economists measure and use, such as "unemployment" and "inflation"; and (2) What do you read to "keep up" with current developments?

This Reader's Guide is an attempt to answer these questions: by the same token it is *not* an attempt to provide a list of supplementary readings for each chapter in this book.

Basic Works

Two basic texts are available which are readable and highly current because each has been amended and enlarged frequently:

1. *Economics* by Paul A. Samuelson (McGraw-Hill)
2. *Economics* by George L. Bach (Prentice-Hall)

Both books cover all of the concepts used by economists, both include a description and documentation of relatively recent data, and both apply the tools of economic thought, not only to the traditional issues usually encompassed by economics but also to current issues such as "population growth," the "quality of life," the "urban crisis," the economics of the "military-industrial complex," and "black capitalism." Both texts are highly readable.

Current Information: Annual Volumes

1. **General economics.** The *Annual Economic Report of the President and the Council of Economic Advisers* (Government Printing Office), available each February, provides an excellent official summary of current and expectable developments in all major aspects of the U.S. economy. In addition, it provides a comprehensive statistical appendix which traces most economic and financial data series back to 1929. From time to time it provides insights into problems that are likely to emerge in the future, as well as clues to current thinking on how they should be resolved.

2. **Monetary matters.** For those more interested in the monetary, banking, and interest rate aspects of economic events, the *Annual Report of the Board of Governors of the Federal Reserve System* provides a readable and definitive analysis of recent developments—both economic and monetary.

3. **International economics.** Developments in our economic relationships, which are covered in summary fashion in both of the Reports cited earlier, are covered in greater detail in three other annual reports.

(a) *The Annual Report of the Council on International Economic Policy (CIEP)*, available from the Government Printing Office.

(b) *The Annual Report of the International Monetary Fund* (Washington, D.C.).

(c) *The Annual Report of the Bank for International Settlement*, Basel, Switzerland, which is especially good on questions relating to the Euro-dollar market.

Current Information: Monthly

Several *monthly* magazines, official and unofficial, provide valuable insights—among them are:

1. *The Survey of Current Business*: The official monthly publication of the U.S. Department of Commerce in which primary statistics on some of our most important economic series, such as National Income, Gross National Product, and Balance of Payments, are presented and analyzed.

2. *The Federal Reserve Bulletin*: The official publication of the Federal Reserve System, in which primary statistics on our major monetary, banking, and interest-rate series are presented, developed, and analyzed.

3. Among the private monthly publications, *Fortune* magazine contains an excellent analysis of the economic situation each month, along with special articles that are written with care for both accuracy and insight.

The monthly newsletter published by the First National City Bank of New York is equally reliable and frequently more interesting.

Current Information: Weekly

The week has become a major cycle in our modern life and reading. A large number of economic publications are available on a seven-day cycle.

1. A subscription to the montly *Survey of Current Business*, referred to earlier, brings a free weekly statistical summary of the most recent facts.

2. *Business Week, U.S. News & World Report, Newsweek,* and *Time*

are widely read by economists. A regular subscription to the *Economist* (a London weekly) provides a complete weekly overview of U.S. as well as international developments.

Current Information: Daily

The Wall Street Journal is by far the outstanding economic daily paper available before breakfast in most U.S. cities.

If I had to pick just *three* private publications I would choose the *Journal*, the *Economist*, and *Business Week*. People who live in the New York area might argue for the *Journal of Commerce* (daily) and the *New York Times*. Both provide an excellent coverage of economic events, but neither is available outside the New York area as rapidly as the *Wall Street Journal*.

ABOUT THE AUTHOR

EZRA SOLOMON WAS BORN and raised in Burma, receiving an honors degree in economics from the University of Rangoon in 1940. When the Japanese Army occupied Burma, Solomon and his family fled into India, where he joined the Burma division of the British Royal Navy. After four years of active service, he was commander of a gunboat, when a long-dormant fellowship for overseas graduate study materialized, and brought him to the University of Chicago in 1947 as a Burma State Scholar. While working toward his PhD at Chicago, awarded in 1950, he joined the faculty of its Graduate School of Business, and was professor of finance from 1956 to 1960.

He has been at Stanford since 1961, when he was invited to be founding director of the International Center for the Advancement of Management Education. After the Center was established and running, Solomon returned to full-time teaching and research as Dean Witter Professor of Finance in the Stanford Graduate School of Business—a position he still holds. In June 1971, he accepted a Presidential appointment in Washington, D.C., as a member of the three-man Council of Economic Advisers, returning to Stanford in March of 1973.

Professor Solomon's expertise in the field of finance and economic policy has earned him visiting professorships in 12 foreign countries, and he has served as a consulting economist to government and industry here and abroad. He has written extensively, and his best-known work, *The Theory of Financial Management*, is widely acknowledged as having had a major impact on the field both in the U.S. and abroad.

He lives on the Stanford campus with his wife, Janet Cameron, and his three daughters, Shan, Ming, and Lorna.

INDEX

Foreign aid, 6
Foreign policy, 6-7
Franklin National Bank, 77

Germany, West, 19, 42, 45-46, 47
GNP, 12-13, 71
Gold and dollars, 4, 47-48
Growth, assumption of, 8

Industrial production (1972-1973),
    boom in, 59, 60, 62-63
Inflation
    composition of (1973-1974), 65-68
    current, 1, 19ff
    historical, 13, 19
    monetary (demand-pull) expla-
        nation of, 21-23, 29-33, 63-67
    and price indices, 64-67
    and recession, 78
    socio-political explanation of,
        24-26
    structural (cost-push) explanation
        of, 26-33, 63-67
Interest rates, 2, 3, 23
Interwar period
    economic performance during, 13
    unemployment during, 8
Investment controls, 40

Japan, resistance to currency
    revaluation, 39-40

Kennedy, John F., 13
Keynes, John Maynard, 8, 11
Keynesian economics, 8-11
Knight, Frank, 15
Kondratieff cycle, 74-75
Korean War, 13

Malthus, Thomas, 10-11
Monetary policy and recession, 80
Monetary system, international, 2,
    35ff
Money supply
    and inflation, 21-23
    worldwide expansion of, 38, 40-49,
        61-62

National Bureau of Economic
    Research, 69

Natural gas
    price ceilings on, 14, 96-98
    supply of, 95ff
Nixon, Richard, 25

Oil
    embargo on, 63, 70, 87
    price of, 2, 7, 63, 73-74, 88ff
OPEC, 89, 91, 100-105
    divisions within, 102-104

Peel, Robert, 17
Penn-Central Railroad, 41, 77
Petrodollars, 2, 73-74, 91-92
Political instability, current, 3
Postwar era
    assumptions of, 2-3
    economic performance during, 13
    economic policy during, 12-15
    end of, 5
    foreign policy during, 6-7
Pre-World War I period, economic
    performance during, 13
Price controls. See Controls
Price indices and inflation, 64-67
Price stability as goal, 13
Productivity, 28-29, 52-53
Public sector of economy, 16

Recession, 69ff
    current, 1, 70-85
    historical, 13, 78-79
Revenue Act of 1932, 75

Saudi Arabia, 90-91, 103-104
Shortages of raw materials, 2
Smithsonian agreement, 48-49, 61
Speculation on currency revaluations,
    44
Stagflation, 69
Stock prices, 2, 3, 107ff
Supply
    and growth, 8-9
    and inflation, 63-67

Taxes. See Fiscal policy
Trade account, 6, 38, 40-41
Trade with Communist nations, 7